C. W. Wing's drawing of the West Cliff c.1810 showing some of the characteristic Brighton hog-boats such as *Ann*, *Venus* and *Jane*. Above the boats can be seen the old *Star and Garter Inn* dating from c.1760 and still in use.

BRIGHTON
A Pictorial History

Dr. Richard Russell F.R.S. (1687-1759), founder of Brighton as a health resort in 1750. Born in Lewes, he set up a practice on the Steine in 1754, and his work *Dissertation on the Use of Sea Water in Diseases of the Glands* (1752) became the handbook for all those seeking the sea-water cure. This portrait by Benjamin Wilson (formerly ascribed to Zoffany and now in Brighton Museum) was for many years displayed in the Old Ship Assembly Rooms and is thought to have been commissioned by a former proprietor, William Hicks.

BRIGHTON
A Pictorial History

D. Robert Elleray, A.L.A.

Fellow of the Royal Society of Arts

Phillimore

1987

Published by
PHILLIMORE & CO. LTD.
Shopwyke Hall, Chichester, Sussex

ISBN 0 85033 627 9

Printed and bound in Great Britain by
BIDDLES LTD., Guildford, Surrey

List of Illustrations

Frontispiece: Portrait of Dr. Richard Russell F.R.S.

For James S. Gray, Brighton historian

Preface

It was my good fortune to have been born in Brighton and for this reason it holds a very special place in my affections – reason enough, I hope, to produce yet another book about the town. The following pages seek to give a modest 'aide-memoire' to those interested in the history of Brighton up to the present, supplemented by illustrations which I hope will give some idea of the visual impact that the town makes on the enthusiastic visitor. It is the evocative and nostalgic nature of such images that together constitute the essence of the place, and the pattern made in the case of Brighton is of absorbing interest and, I hope, will move the reader to enjoy more fully the wonderful town of Brighton.

The literature on Brighton is considerable, and Dr. Sue Farrant's *Guide to printed sources ... of Brighton* (1977) is a useful introduction. Recommended basic books are: Antony Dale, *Fashionable Brighton 1820-1860* (1947, 1967); Jill and John Ford, *Images of Brighton* (1981); Edmund Gilbert, *Brighton, old ocean's bauble* (1954, 1975); Clifford Musgrave, *Life in Brighton* (1970, 1981); and Osbert Sitwell and Margaret Barton, *Brighton* (1935). On the Royal Pavilion, the following are particularly recommended: John Dinkel, *The Royal Pavilion* (1983); John Morley, *The Making of the Royal Pavilion, Brighton* (1984); and Henry Roberts, *The Royal Pavilion* (1939).

D. Robert Elleray
1987

Acknowledgements

Most of the illustrative material in this book has come from the author's own collection which includes material from the late Henfrey Smail's collection. Many of the photographs have been taken by the author and the photographic work has been carried out by David Nicholls (Worthing).

I am most grateful to the following for permission to reproduce illustrations: The County Librarian, East Sussex County Library; Messrs. Holleyman & Treacher, booksellers (Brighton); The Brighton Philharmonic Society; James S. Gray; Messrs. Duckworth & Co. Ltd., Publishers (for the John Piper drawing); the Brighton Borough Plan Registry; Dr. P. Connor (Brighton Museum) for the portrait of Dr. Russell; The National Monuments Record (Crown Copyright Reserved), illustrations nos. 77 and 110; Norman Read; C. A. Morris, A.R.W.S.; and R. Stent.

I am also indebted to the following for their kind assistance in writing the book: James S. Gray; Caroline Jacob and the staff of Brighton Reference Library; and the generous help given by Mr. P. Pedrick of the Brighton Borough Plan Registry. I am especially grateful for the help of Miss Esme Evans, B.A., A.L.A., for typing the manuscript and captions.

[Brighton], which in the memory of our grandfathers was only a small insignificant town, on a corner of the coast little frequented, has now become fashionable, elegant, and universally known. Till lately it had the name of Brighthelmstone; but, like low persons rising to eminence, who are often ashamed of their origin, it has now assumed the title of Brighton; which certainly has a more genteel sound, and 'passes trippingly o'er the tongue'.

A Guide to all the Watering Places and Sea-Bathing Places for 1813

Brighton is the most convenient spot in all the south-eastern part of the Kingdom, when in search of 'a lark', and a great recommendation that is.

New Monthly Magazine, 1841

There are some who say that Brighton is one of the two most beautiful towns in the land. Even those who do not rate it so highly will agree that Brighton front, with its long line of stuccoed houses, with their bright paint not marred by grime and smoke, with their bow-windows and hooded balconies, and the Downs rising behind the town, is one of the loveliest urban scenes in England.

Edmund W. Gilbert, *Brighton: Old Ocean's Bauble*, 1954

Introduction

The Early Town

Brighton[1] belongs to that category of seaside resort which developed on the site of an old community, rather than springing into existence mushroom-like in the open countryside. At the time of the Norman Conquest Brighton comprised three manors[2] originally belonging to Earl Godwin, and subsequently appearing in Domesday. In 1080 a Friary of St Bartholomew was founded in the area of the present Town Hall and an ancient church of Saxon origin, dedicated to St Nicholas, and later rebuilt in the 14th century, occupied a relatively remote site to the north-west, not to be engulfed by urban growth until well into the 19th century. A constable was appointed in 1285, a market charter was granted in 1312, and by 1500 a sea wall rather similar to one at Hastings had been erected as a deterrent to French coastal raiders. Such emergencies arose in 1514 and 1545.

Radulf͛ ten͛ de Willo *BRISTELMESTVNE*. Briƈtric
tenuit de dono Goduini. T.R.E 7 m̃ ſe defđ ᵽ.v. hiđ
7 dimiđ. T̃ra.ē.III.caī. In dñio.ē dim̃ caī.7 xvIII.uilłi
7 IX.borđ.cũ.III.caī.7 uno ſeruo. De gablo.IIII.mil alleciũ.
T.R.E.ualb vIII.lib 7 xII.ſol.7 poſt:́c.ſol. Modo:́xII.lib.

Ralph holds BRIGHTON from William. Brictric held it by gift of Earl Godwin. Before 1066 and now it answered for 5½ hides.
Land for 3 ploughs. In lordship ½ plough;
    18 villagers and 9 smallholders with 3 ploughs and 1 slave.
    From tribute 4,000 herrings.
Value before 1066 £8 12s; later 100s; now £12.

1. The Domesday entry for Brighton.

The French attack of 1514 resulted in the burning of the town and was a major disaster, apparently destroying the Friary and nearly all the timber building, but leaving the church unharmed. Ironically this unhappy event produced a benefit for the historian – a drawing of the attack which provides the first evidence of Brighton's appearance at this early date. The sketch clearly shows a small town contained in a rectangle bounded by the sea, West, North and East streets. Middle Street and the Lanes, which had and still retain a huddled medieval configuration, lay within this modest area. Between East Street and the Welsbourne stream extended an open area or common, the Steine[3], later to become a focus for visitors, but traditionally used by the fishing community for net drying and repair. Until the opening of the 18th century there existed[4] a 'lower town' situated to the south beneath an eroding chalk cliff, and a hint of this area, which may well have been the original fishing community, is shown in the drawing.

In 1665 serious storm damage was sustained and the area finally succumbed in 1705 when the waves overwhelmed it; by the end of the century the 'Town House' together with a blockhouse (1558) and protecting wall had also vanished. Towards the end of the 16th century, in spite of sea encroachment Brighton had developed as a herring fishing community and a measure of prosperity is suggested by the estimate that there were some eighty fishing-boats in use employing 400 mariners with 10,000 nets. To ensure that a fair levy of taxes was made on all inhabitants, both landsmen and mariners, the first unit of local government was appointed – 'The Twelve' – composed of 'the ancientist, gravest and wisest inhabitants, eight fishermen and fawer landsmen for assistants to the Constable in every public cause'. A number of ordinances resulting from the Twelve's deliberations were published as *The Book of All the Auncient Customs*, dated 23 July 1580.

By the close of the 17th century mackerel fishing had been profitably introduced, and an important local design of boat was evolved, the 'Hog-boat', with a broad beam and versatile manoeuverability, specially adapted to conditions on the Brighton beaches. The prosperity of the fishing trade declined during the second quarter of the 18th century, and by this time the erosion of the lower town had forced the community to transfer to the higher areas and thus to impinge on the landsmen who were mainly farmers, deriving a livelihood from the five great fields known as 'tenantry laines'[5] situated around the perimeter of the town. These lands became subject to speculative development towards the end of the 18th century, and their system of subdivision later influenced the pattern of street formation.

There was a considerable lapse of time following the early 16th-century sketch of Brighton until further views and prospects were produced providing evidence of the town's changing appearance. A *Perspective View* by James Lambert (1765) gives an interesting vista of the eastern side of Brighton clearly showing the Steine and the buildings on its west side. C. Lampriere's *South View of Brighton* (1743) in Relhan's *Short History* (1829), and the *View of Brighthelmstone in Sussex*, engraved for Walpole's *New and Complete British Traveller* in 1784, still show a town standing *by* the sea but not yet looking *towards* it for anything more than a source of livelihood for a small fishing community. But even as the second of these views was being made, a significant change of attitude towards the sea had already begun; doctors were recommending salt water as a means of curing disease, Dr. Russell had established a practice on the Steine and a fashionable interest in the sea was emerging which led to the new resort architecture of Brighton assuming a grand facade overlooking the object of benefit to both residents and visitors – the ocean.

Dr. Richard Russell and the Sea-Water Cure
The undisputed founder of modern Brighton was Dr. Richard Russell; without Russell there would have been no visiting royalty, and in particular, no Prince Regent. The town's debt to the Doctor is immense, and the absence of a fitting memorial to him a matter of surprise, the plaque attached to the *Royal Albion Hotel* being totally inadequate.

In 1750 Dr. Russell, who practised in Lewes, began sending patients to Brighton to try a sea-water cure, the experiment proving so successful that three years later he decided to establish a practice in the town. His house – Russell House – at the south end of the Steine, was later to be rented by the Duke of Cumberland, and finally replaced by the *Royal Albion Hotel*. Russell's research and practice concerning the beneficial use of sea-water culminated in an important book, the *Dissertation on the Use of Sea Water in Diseases of the Glands* (1750),[6] which remained for several years the standard handbook on the treatment, stocked in all the circulating libraries of Brighton, where the book was referred to by everyone as 'Russell on Sea-water'.[7] Once the flow of health seekers to Brighton had been set in motion by the cure, it steadily increased and soon included important people – the Thrales, Fanny Burney, Dr. Johnson, Sir John and Lady Shelley and even John Wilkes. In July 1765 royalty first arrived in the person of the Duke of Gloucester, who soon patronised the *Castle Inn* Assembly Rooms and was received by Thomas Pelham at Stanmer House. The small town's response to the growing number of visitors was slow and it was not until the 1760s that efforts began to be made to erect larger houses and enhance older ones. The facilities for the actual 'dipping' of visitors in the sea also expanded with growing numbers of bathing machines under the guidance of that great Brighton character the 'dipper' Martha Gunn and her male counterpart, the 'bather' 'Smoaker' Miles.

Following the death of Dr. Russell in 1759, a number of physicians attempted to continue his work, and one, an Irishman, Anthony Relhan, may be considered his successor. Relhan, like Russell, prescribed both immersion in, and drinking of, sea-water, together with relaxation, but extended the cure to emphasise the importance of sea air.[8] Also following in the Russell tradition was Dr. John Awsiter, who was especially important as the promoter of indoor bathing, which quickly led to the development of covered baths to mitigate the frequently harsh conditions experienced on Brighton's exposed and shingly beaches. In the absence of any public move to act upon his advice Awsiter erected his own baths the following year, designed by Robert Golden[9], where warm water treatment and massaging also became part of the routine. The baths were just to the south-west of Pool Valley where they continued with various alterations and changes of name until the late 1920s when the Savoy Cinema was built on the site[10]. Covered baths for swimming were a later development and the first was opened on the site of the old East Battery in 1823 by Lamprell, later becoming Brill's.

Dr. Russell had also discovered the chalybeate spring in what is now St Ann's Well Gardens, Hove, and enclosed it making the waters part of his recommended treatment. Much later in 1825 the fashionable craving for taking the waters was catered for by a German, Dr. Frederick Struve, who established the Royal German Spa at the south end of Queen's Park where a range of imitation mineral waters such as Ems, Kesselbrunnen and Seltzer were dispensed in a small Pump Room to distinguished visitors including William IV and Queen Adelaide. It was an Indian, however, who is remembered as the most colourful promoter of health in Brighton – Sake Deen Mahomed. He arrived from Patna via Cork complete with an Irish wife and established Mahomed's Warm, Cold and Vapour Baths (1786), on a site now occupied by the *Queen's Hotel*. Shampooing (i.e. massaging) was a speciality but the forte was a medicated steam, or vapour bath, in which the patient was allowed to sweat freely inside a flannel tent filled with steam. The technique impressed the medical profession, including Dr. John Gibney, Senior Physician at the Royal Sussex County Hospital. Mahomed's success was considerable; in 1822 he published a popular handbook *Shampooing* ... and subsequently gained the singular honour of being appointed 'Shampooing Surgeon to His Majesty King George IV' – a title which meant that Mahomed was in charge of the royal bathroom at the Pavilion!

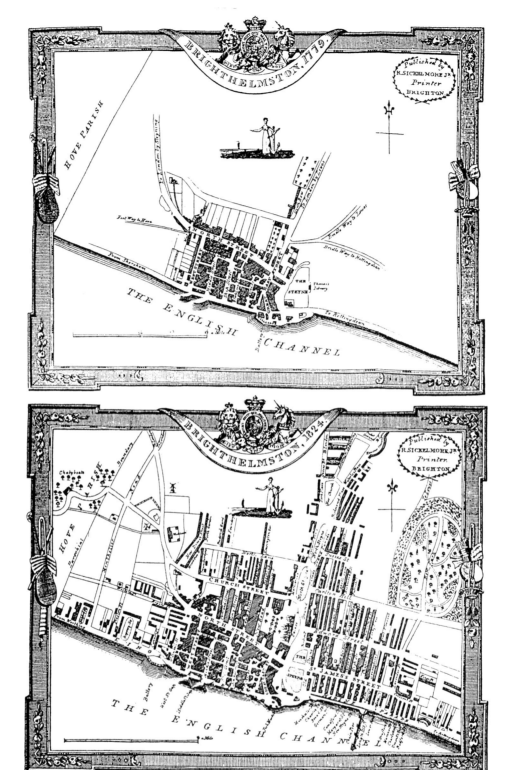

2. Two early maps of Brighton showing the extraordinary growth achieved between 1779 and 1824, when the population leapt from some 2,700 to about 25,000, and the small fishing town formerly contained within the limits of East, North and West Streets suddenly became a fashionable Regency resort.

Unlike Worthing, Brighton's beach was not a comfortable or particularly safe location for the cure, there were pebbles not sand; deep, often rough, water, not shallow calm: the town became a leading seaside resort as a social and fashionable centre, rather than as an idyllic environment. Royalty had promoted Bath as the premier spa; Brighton then experienced a similar benefit but with two telling advantages – its proximity to London and the regular presence of the Court. The cure had psychological as well as physical attraction: as Antony Dale comments[11] 'Society in every age has always delighted to be recommended by its medical advisers to resort to just those places which it was determined in any case to visit, with or without the appropriate symptoms'. So Brighton eclipsed Bath, the Duke of Gloucester arrived in 1765, and the following year the *Castle Inn* on the Steine judged the future secure enough to erect a ballroom, as did the *Ship Inn* in 1767. The basic requisites for the establishment of company life appeared with the first libraries, a theatre and subsequently chapels of ease to the parish church. In 1793 the Promenade Grove, a miniature Vauxhall, had been laid out in the area now occupied by New Street, and provided a fashionable rendezvous for visitors until the expansion of the Pavilion led to its closure nine years later.

In September 1783 the Prince of Wales arrived to stay with his uncle, the Duke of Gloucester, and apparently liking what he found, returned the following year – it seems on the advice of the royal doctors who recommended sea-bathing as a remedy for his swollen neck glands. With the Prince installed at Brighton, the resort became a magnet drawing an increasing number of upper-class visitors, but also attracted undesirable elements, some of these raffish cronies of the Prince, whose behaviour often scandalised both residents and older visitors. To this mixture was added a sizeable ingredient of garrison troops stationed in the south-east during the Napoleonic emergency, which also brought emigré Frenchmen, who frequently found the new Brighton society much to their taste. In addition to the *Ship* and *Castle* assembly rooms and the popular circulating libraries, the Steine, which had been levelled, and the Pool, drained in 1792, provided the main focus of fashionable society in Brighton, especially during the opening decade of the 19th century – 'It was the place to which all resorted and where all comingled'.[12] The fine aquatint by Cracklow and Craig (1806) provides an informative glimpse of the 'promenade', and includes the Prince and Martha Gunn. Around the Steine notable buildings soon began to increase – the *Castle Tavern*, Marlborough House, Steine House, the residence of Mrs. Fitzherbert, and the first libraries: Baker's, rebuilt as Donaldson's in 1806, now the south corner of St James's Street, and Woodgate's, later Widgett's, etc. near the present *Royal York Hotel*. Adjacent to the Steine in Castle Square were the main coach offices where in 1822 some sixty-two coaches left every day for London. Later, in the mid-1820s, the popularity of the Steine gave way to the new attraction of the Chain Pier, where the large flagged promenade at the head became a popular rendezvous.

The Royal Pavilion and Regency Architecture

Perhaps the most significant feature of the Regency in Brighton was the Prince's wide interest in the arts and building which soon led to the influence of fashionable architects such as Holland and Nash being felt in the town. When the young Prince Regent first came to Brighton he stayed at Grove House, built on a site now occupied

LEWES, *Sept. 8.*

Yesterday his Royal Highness the Prince of Wales' arrived at Brighthelmston at dinner, on a visit to their Royal Highnesses the Duke and Duchess of Cumberland; and we have it from undoubted authority that his Royal Highness intends being at the BALL, at SHERGOLD's this evening, which will be a Dress Ball, without Hats, in compliment to his Royal Highness.

About half after two, his Royal Highness's arrival was announced by the ringing of bells, and a royal salute from the guns at the battery, when unhappily, thro' some indiscetion in re-loading one of the pieces, it went off, and wounded the under gunner so mortally, that he died in a very short time afterwards. His body was blown off the battery, to some distance on the beach, and one of his arms shattered to pieces, the middle part of which was taken up, but his hand, it is supposed, was blown into the sea, as it could not be found.

It is remarkable that an accident of the like nature happened last year at Brighthelmston, on the Princess Amelia's visiting that place, when the gunner, by one of the guns unexpectedly going off, had his hand blown to pieces, and was otherwise so much wounded, that his life was for a considerable time in great danger.

The Duke of Cumberland, on being acquainted with the above melancholy accident, expressed great concern, and on enquiry found that the unfortunate man had left a widow behind him, for whom, there is not the least doubt, an ample provision will be made.

About half after six, the Heir Apparent, and his royal uncle the Duke of Cumberland, appeared on the Steine, where their Highnesses walked about half an hour, and then went to the rooms.

It being Sunday evening, the Steine was thronged with *company*, who flocked in motley groupes to see the Royal Guest.

The town and Steine were illuminated, and the brilliancy of the evening concluded by a grand display of fire-works before the Duke of Cumberland's house.

The Prince of Wales, it is thought, will return to town on Tuesday.

3. The *Sussex Weekly Advertiser's* historic announcement of the arrival of the Prince of Wales in Brighton on 8 September 1783 to visit his uncle the Duke of Cumberland.

by the north-east corner of the Pavilion, and in 1786 a farmhouse close by, owned by Thomas Read Kemp and leased to Louis Weltje (later the Prince's cook and major-domo), was acquired by the Prince in 1786 as a residence, and at once remodelled as the 'Marine Pavilion' by Henry Holland. Additions followed in 1801-3, and at about this time Chinese interior decorations were introduced. In 1803-4 William Porden was commissioned by the Prince to erect stables and a riding house (since 1868 the Corn Exchange) to the north-west of the Pavilion, the great domed stables first bringing the 'Indian' style into the town. The 'Dome', as it became called, so impressed the Prince that he commissioned Humphrey Repton to rebuild the Marine Pavilion in a matching style, but the project never materialised because of financial difficulties, and it was not until 1815 that the Prince Regent appointed John Nash to build a new palace, thus giving Brighton one of the most fanciful and extraordinary buildings in Europe. The project was completed in 1820, and the next year the adjacent *Castle Inn* ballroom was acquired for conversion into a Royal

4. His Majesty George IV on his accession to the throne, from a print published by Henry Colburn in 1820. As Prince Regent, he gave lasting fame to Brighton as a resort after his arrival in September 1783. The Prince first occupied Grove House, and then the Marine Pavilion, commissioned from Henry Holland in 1787. George IV's last visit to Brighton extended from January until 7 March 1827, ending an association with the town of nearly 44 years.

5. Maria Anne Smythe (1756-1837), later Mrs. Fitzherbert, was twice married before her unhappy association with the Prince Regent, first to Edmond Weld and then to Thomas Fitzherbert who died in 1778. Although a Roman Catholic, Mrs. Fitzherbert and the Prince were married secretly on 21 December 1785 – an invalid union which allowed George to marry Caroline of Brunswick in 1795. In 1803 Mrs. Fitzherbert withdrew from Court on a pension of £6,000 a year and lived in her house on the Steine until her death.

Chapel. The east facade of the new Pavilion still retains traces of Holland's original layout and this transformation process is indicated in plates 14-16. Inside, much of the original furniture was designed by Holland and the decor executed by Frederick and John Crace, and Robert Jones – the climax being reached in the truly exquisite Music Room, damaged by fire in 1975, and since then so wonderfully restored. When the Pavilion was secured by the town in 1850 (by referendum with a majority of only 36 votes out of a poll of 2650) the furniture and many fittings were removed. Much later, just after the Second World War, it was resolved to revive the former glory of the palace and much of the original furniture was returned for the Regency Exhibitions of subsequent years.

The erection of Royal Crescent at the turn of the 18th century marks the opening of a remarkable period of Regency architecture in Brighton which lasted some forty years and influenced the style of building in the town until around 1860. The climax of this great speculative boom fell in the 1820s, when a small group of local architects inspired, and occasionally supplemented, by others of national reputation, created a legacy of more than provincial importance. The period of intense activity began with the arrival in 1820 of the talented Charles Augustus Busby who had published in 1807 *A Series of Designs for Villas and Country Houses ...* , which had some influence on the stylistic development of domestic houses and in particular on the introduction of stucco moulding and bold semi-circular bays, the style which became so typical of the Brighton Regency townscape. Busby soon formed a partnership with Amon Wilds who had come to Brighton from Lewes some five years before with his son Amon Henry, and the outstanding achievement of their association was the design of one of the most striking Regency estates – Kemp Town – a Nash-inspired speculation by the rich Thomas Read Kemp begun in 1823, but never completed in full. A notable feature was St George's Chapel, designed by Busby in 1824. The partnership employed Thomas Cubitt as builder, and both Kemp and Cubitt lived for a time in the estate, at 22 Sussex Square and 13 Lewes Crescent respectively. In 1834 Kemp Town inspired Brunswick Town in West Brighton, this time a speculation by Thomas White Scutt on his Wick Farm Estate, possibly promoted by Wilds and Busby. Brunswick Square displays particularly fine examples of Greek Revival detailing, and the estate was provided with a market (later used as a riding school, and more recently the short-lived OMAC Arts Centre) and a fine chapel, St Andrew's, Waterloo Street (1827-8) by Charles Barry. In 1832 Busby was appointed Surveyor to Brunswick Town, a post he held for only three years before his early death in 1834. Amon Wilds tended to be overshadowed by the qualified Busby, but before 1822 he designed several buildings and introduced his firm's device – the 'Ammonite' capital in the form of the fossil – apparently a pun on his name. Of particular interest was Western Lodge (1817), a pinnacled Gothick design in stucco, a small part of which survives above the north-east corner of Debenham's store in Western Road. Some two years before, Amon Wilds had designed Richmond and Waterloo Places, near St Peter's church.[13] Waterloo Place was of particular interest for the attractive combination of buff brick and stucco enriched with pilasters, bays and verandahs. It seems incredible that this fine Regency terrace in the curtiledge of St Peter's should have been sacrificed for harsh concrete and glass in 1968-70.[14] Amon Wilds became Surveyor to the Brighton Commissioners from 1825-28.

Amon Henry Wilds began an independent practice following the formation of his father's partnership, and contributed much to the Regency-style architecture of

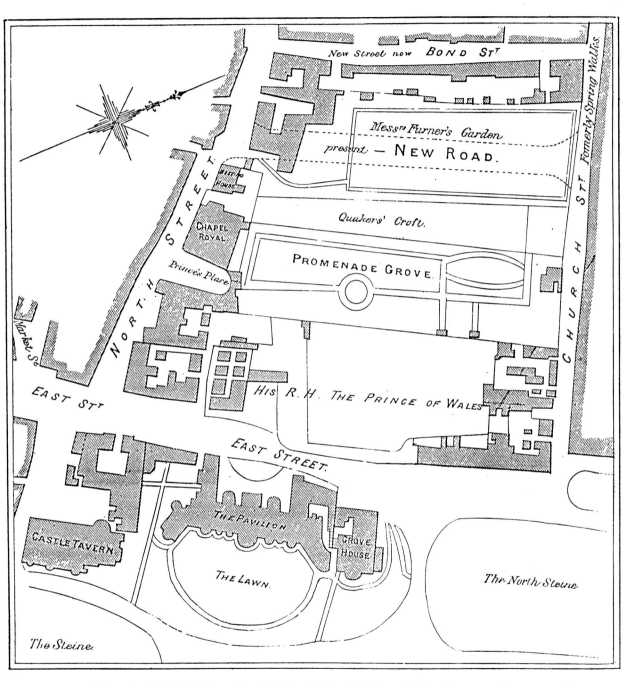

6. An 1803 plan showing Holland's original Marine Pavilion (1787) and indicating some of the proposed changes necessitated by the Prince Regent's enlargement scheme. The 'Proposed New Road' compensated for the cutting-short of East Street as a public road, and 'Promenade Grove', which had opened in 1793 as a pleasure garden, had been purchased by the Prince in 1802.

Brighton, occupying his own miniature 'Pavilion' in Western Terrace, where he also designed Silwood Place and House, Western Terrace and nearby Oriental Place. Other notable works include the Royal Newburgh Assembly Rooms, Cannon Place (*c*.1827); Hanover Crescent (1827), with its delightful lodges; Park Crescent (1829), where the new Italianate influence was evident; and Montpellier Crescent (1843-47), an excellent example of the persistence of the Regency style well beyond its nominal period. Thomas Cooper, a builder architect, played his part in the Regency expansion of Brighton and is best remembered for the old *Bedford Hotel* (1829), demolished in 1965, and the present Town Hall (1830).

Two years after the completion of Brunswick Town another portion of the Wick Farm Estate was proposed by Thomas Read Kemp as a western pendant to Kemp Town, but Kemp's worsening financial position forbade this, and he sold the land to Sir Isaac Lyon Goldsmid, who later became the first Jewish Baronet (Palmeira). The development, at first named Queen Adelaide Crescent, began in December 1830. with Goldsmid employing Decimus Burton who, with his father, James, was then building the new town of St Leonards-on-Sea at Hastings. For unexplained reasons the project faltered after the erection of only the south-east corner and part of the east side, and thereafter languished until 1850 when the rest was completed by an unknown architect. The difference in the two wings says much about the change of style during the intervening years, resulting in Greek revival on most of the Burton side and Italianate on the other. Palmeira Square completed the estate (1855-70) in a vigorous Italianate style remote from the original Regency conception, but dignified in its formal parkland setting. The estate chapel of St John the Baptist was built nearby on a site given by Goldsmid in 1852.

7.   Print of about 1815 of West Cliff showing hogboats and bathing machines. Above is the area now occupied by the *Queen's Hotel*.

As already mentioned the sheer momentum of the Regency style in Brighton and Hove carried its use far into the 19th century, leaving many examples of pleasant stucco buildings, some of which have outstanding quality and charm: among these are Belgrave Place by Thomas Cubitt (1846); Powis Square, and especially Clifton Terrace (c.1850) 'the last of the Regency', and nearby Clifton Hill and Clifton Place. Regency Brighton perfected a civilised practice of 'town planning' long before the concept was defined in a later, less civilised, age.

The Railway – Victorian and Edwardian Brighton

> I took the train to Brighton – I walked besides the sea,
> And thirty thousand Londoners were there along with me.
> We crowded every lodging, and we lumbered each hotel,
> Sniffed the briny for an appetite, and dined extremely well.

In the 1840s Brighton made the acquaintance of a new species of visitor – the 'tripper' – and the experience was not entirely a happy one. Elizabeth Cook[15] wrote that the tripper appeared because of 'the growth of railways and monster trains', and Ruskin[16] added later 'the modern tripper leaves only desolation and dirty papers behind him'. The initial impact of the railway opened to Brighton in 1841 was a major increase in holiday traffic, commerce and settlement, which helped to counter the post-Regency slump in the town. Statistics reveal the striking nature of these effects: in the decade 1831-41, 437 houses were built; the next 10 years saw no less than 2,806. The population jumped from 46,000 in 1841 to 65,000 in 1851. The trains brought some 74,000 visitors during May 1850; 11 years later, 132,000 arrived on Easter Monday alone. In these circumstances it is not surprising that the 1851 census remarked 'Seaside resorts have expanded more rapidly than any other group of English towns'.

The newly-discovered mobility of working people meant that Sundays, in spite of Sabbatarianism and the strongly-supported Anti Sunday-Travelling Union, became a gala day and the accepted occasion for mass pleasure-seeking migrations to the seaside. By 1860 the resorts had become a major feature of Victorian social life and the introduction of the August 'Bank Holiday' in 1871 completed this new social pattern. 'The excursion train',[17] comments Clifford Musgrave[18] '... brought about the downfall of Brighton as an exclusive resort of the wealthy and fashionable society, and its rebirth as the truly democratic pleasure resort of modern times'. This, however, was also true of other places. What the railway gave Brighton, in addition, was the establishment in 1852 of a significant resident colony of railway workers. This, together with other railway labourers and the growing number of service industry employees, meant that Brighton began to possess an above-average working-class element in its population, with attendant poverty, slum areas and health problems, and eventually political consequences. The presence of this 'other Brighton' as opposed to the 'fashionable image' is evident in Ruff's print *The Railway Terminus and St Peter's Church ...*, c.1850, where smoking chimneys and serried ranks of housing make their appearance in striking contrast to the normal 19th-century views of the town. This industrial presence, begun by the railways, was to colour the development of Brighton and much later aggravated labour unrest during the General Strike.

By the third quarter of the 19th century both the urban and cosmopolitan character of Brighton had become well established and 'London-by-the-Sea' began to provide the range of entertainment normally expected by a growing clientele of holidaymakers. The great success of the Theatre Royal under the direction of Mr. and Mrs. Nye Chart brought the town notoriety as a theatre centre, easy rail travel facilitating 'flying matinee' visits to the resort. The West Pier opened in 1866, the Aquarium in 1872, to which were added Volk's Electric Railway in 1883 and the imaginative improvement of the Madeira Drive area. Finally the ageing Chain Pier was replaced by the splendid new Palace Pier, which was the ultimate in pier design and became the most spectacular single attraction in Brighton. On shore the social importance of the Steine was by mid-century eclipsed by the King's Road, where the *beau monde* paraded, albeit progressively diluted by elements from the lower strata of the social scale, the focal point being the bottom of West Street, where the main thrust of trippers surged down in vast numbers from the railway station.

On Sundays the visiting crowds were confronted by one of Brighton's spectacles – the 'church parade' – numerous fashionable people who had chosen to attend 'Mattins' rather than 'Muttons'[19] to pass their Sunday morning and thereafter to stroll along the King's Road. In Brighton at this period[20] there were 38 churches and chapels, over 24,000 sittings and 36,573 was an average Sunday attendance. The local clash between 'High' and 'Low' churches began with the opening of St Paul's, West Street, in 1848, built by the Wagner family, whose considerable fortune promoted the High Church cause in the town and led to over fifty years of controversy[21]. Preaching also became a highly fashionable attraction with Joseph Sortain, J. B. Figgis, James Vaughan, and especially F. W. Robertson during his brief encumbency at Holy Trinity, Ship Street, in 1847-53. The great efforts to provide accommodation for visitors and residents led to a rich flowering of church building in Brighton with contributions from some leading 19th-century achitects, but it was a local man, Edmund Scott, who designed St Bartholomew's, Ann Street in 1874, one of the most impressive 19th-century churches in Britain. The town's legacy of churches resulting from these events still forms one of the most important elements in Brighton's architecture and has more than local interest.

By 1901 the combined population of Brighton and Hove had reached 160,000, but thereafter expansion slowed considerably. In spite of the great success of the first London to Brighton motorcar runs, there were distinct signs of stagnation, such as the derelict state of certain sea front buildings and, above all, the delay in completing the Palace Pier undoubtedly indicating a faltering in Brighton's progress. A renewal of fashionable impetus was needed. The presence of an important Jewish family, the Sassoons, in the 1870s helped to revive grand connections when a number of their friends, and members of the English royal family, began to visit the town. In 1908-9 Edward VII visited Brighton three times, staying with his daughter, Princess Louise, Duchess of Fife, at 1 Lewes Crescent. The King returned in 1910, and as a result Brighton experienced a sharp revival of its fashionable reputation. The arrival of Harry Preston in 1901 to manage the *Royal York Hotel* provided Brighton with a popular and dynamic character who dedicated the rest of his life to reviving the town's status as a leading resort. Preston's great enthusiasm for sport coincided with a growing interest in football. Brighton and Hove Albion Football Club was founded in 1902, and the Sussex County Cricket ground, established on its present site in 1872 was a further source of attraction for the town. A much-admired figure in Brighton, Sir Harry remained a resident until his death in 1936, and the use of his hotels by a long succession of prominent people led to a return of the town's reputation as a top resort and resulted in prosperous conditions being maintained in spite of war, strikes and the general depression then prevailing in the country.

Modern Brighton, 1914–

During the First World War Brighton enjoyed comparative prosperity; restrictions on travel abroad increased the number of tourists and the town was often full of troops on leave and later war wounded. In several ways the period bore a resemblance to the Napoleonic emergency, when the south-east had prospered because of the presence of garrison troops and fashionable visitors. The years immediately following the War also resembled those experienced after 1815 – a period of slump and decline, although in its efforts to clear slum areas the Council achieved the impressive total of some five hundred houses erected in 1922. In 1910-11 the cinema age had opened in Brighton with the Duke of York's and the Academy (formerly West Street); but the most significant post-war promotion was the erection in 1921 of a major cinema, the Regent, in Queen's Road, which claimed to be Britain's first 'super cinema'. Designed by Robert Atkinson, it remained an important venue in the town's social life for many years. In 1925 the town's musical life was enriched by the founding of the Brighton Philharmonic Players by Herbert Menges, under whose conductorship the group developed into a prominent orchestra, the Brighton Philharmonic, which continues today.

Towards the close of the decade, in May 1928, the Duke of York (later George VI) and his Duchess visited the town and laid the foundation stones of two large pylons

8. A print c.1850 showing Sir Francis Chantrey's statue of George IV in its original position in the Steine, erected by public subscription in 1828. The figure was moved to its present site north of the Pavilion in 1922 to make way for the War Memorial.

marking the entrance to 'Greater Brighton'– the augmented Borough following the addition of Patcham, Falmer, Rottingdean and Ovingdean in that year – an achievement marking a personal triumph for the veteran Alderman Herbert Carden who had received the Freedom of Brighton in 1926 and who was knighted in 1930 for his services to the Borough.

An important element in the comparative prosperity enjoyed in Brighton in the decade running up to the Second World War was the electrification of the railway to London in 1932-33. *Country Life*[22], commenting in January 1933, saw both the advantages and increase in municipal responsibility involved for the town: 'a great influx of permanent residents, such as is bound to occur, only makes it more necessary than ever that the amenities and attractions of Brighton and its surroundings shall be preserved – that there will be no more Peacehavens. Otherwise ... Brighton ... will find that it has once more killed the goose that lays the golden eggs'. Much improvement achieved by the town in the 1930s resulted from the foresight of Herbert Carden, who ensured that large tracts of land around the Borough were secured for future expansion, including a 'green belt'. Slum clearance continued, and attractive new housing estates, especially at Moulscoomb, were carried out during these years. The remodelling of the Aquarium, the construction of the road, sea wall and undercliff walk to Rottingdean were positive evidence of progress and countered the problems of unemployment, as did the continuing boom in cinema building. However, the pressures increased for changes in the historic areas of the town, and what David L. Murray called the 'ferro-concrete age' was at hand.

In 1935 the Borough published a *Royal Jubilee Souvenir*, in which Alderman Sir Herbert Carden[23] indicated his plans for sweeping changes affecting the Regency areas of the town. There was an immediate reaction from *The Sphere* in an article: 'Brighton Threatened: Is London-by-the-Sea to be Robbed of its Regency Charm?' (6 July 1935). According to the Editor, 'Alderman Sir Herbert Carden wishes to transform Brighton ... Sir Herbert, thinking in terms of white concrete and flagpoles, seems to forget there is a Regency Brighton as well, and that a large proportion of the visitors to Brighton go there because of these things'. Apparently it was Embassy Court that inspired Alderman Carden, and he was soon advocating the demolition of the whole of the sea front from Kemp Town to Hove. 'Even Sussex Square will have to go', he said; but that was not all, unfortunate as it may now seem, the Royal Pavilion was also expendable as 'a complete anachronism in a modern age' and just the site for a new conference and entertainment centre! These views drew little criticism, and were also shared by another member of the Council, the young Lewis Cohen (later Lord Cohen of Brighton) who described the Pavilion as 'that bulbous and archaic monstrosity'.[24] In fact, the coming of the war saved Brighton from 'transformation', but the year 1935 saw the first incursions of 'ferro concrete' into the town's most sensitive area – the sea front with the stark Embassy Court[25] overshadowing the delicate proportions of Brunswick Terrace, and later, Marine Gate, above Black Rock. Also typical of the 1930s were the cinemas; the Astoria, Granada, West Street Odeon and Gaiety (all now closed or demolished) representing the film-going boom of the period.

The Second World War proved a far more difficult time for Brighton than the years 1914-1918. For the first time since 1514 the town suffered damage and casualties from enemy action, and during 1940-1942 the imminent threat of invasion. In the autumn of 1939 the population was swollen by the arrival of over thirty thousand evacuees plus considerable numbers of military personnel, but as the war intensified in 1940 a re-evacuation to safer areas was carried out in which local children were included. During the Dunkirk evacuation some twenty local boats took part in the rescue operations and two of the famous Campbell pleasure steamers, the *Brighton Queen* and *Brighton Belle*, were lost during the war. Most of the large hotels were either closed or occupied by the military and R.A.F.; the Hove Baths were taken over by the Navy and the name H.M.S. *King Alfred* remains as a reminder of this wartime use. Roedean School was also commandeered as H.M.S. *Vernon*.

While tourist activity was suspended, the presence of the armed forces ensured prosperity for entertainments, especially for the cinemas, and the Hippodrome and Grand played an important part in lightening the wartime austerity. It was at the Hippodrome that the Brighton music-hall star Max Miller, one of the best-loved comedians of the period, gave many memorable performances. The Dome continued to hold concerts with Herbert Menges and visits from famous orchestras, while the Pavilion fulfilled its great promise as the cultural centrepiece of Brighton's social life.

As Brighton slowly recovered from the deprivations of war attention began to turn towards the future role of the town, and the realisation of the unique nature and value of the Royal Pavilion to Brighton. The crucial change in attitudes towards the Pavilion, from viewing it as a masterpiece rather than a monstrosity, began with the publication of *Brighton* by Margaret Barton and Sir Osbert Sitwell in 1935, and has progressed steadily ever since. Soon after the war, the suggestion, by Professor Sir Charles Reilly that a Regency Festival should be mounted was adopted and carried out with the assistance of Their Majesties King George VI, Queen Elizabeth and Queen Mary. From this success the 'Regency Exhibitions' developed and in 1950,the centenary of the acquisition of the Pavilion, a special Exhibition was opened by the Duke and Duchess of Devonshire, these events obviously influencing the choice of Brighton as one of the 'Festival Towns' held in 1951.

Some of the credit for the new attitude towards the Royal Pavilion was also due to a general realisation of the growing threat to the town's heritage of Regency architecture, and in particular to the statement of Hove Council that its plans to demolish Brunswick Square and Terraces 'would in no way alter the character of the town'! It was to combat these negative tendencies that a meeting was held in December 1945 which resulted in the foundation of the Regency Society to guard against the destruction of the town's historic areas. As Edmund Gilbert has written[26] 'It had become necessary to protect the beauty of Brighton and Hove's squares and terraces' continuing: 'Quite apart from any question of aesthetics, it would be bad business to deprive Brighton of its historic character which makes her the most attractive seaside resort in the country, if not in the world'.

The concept of Brighton and Hove as a 'Regional Capital' began to crystallise between the wars, if not before, and Sir Herbert Carden's ultimate goal was a city stretching from the Adur to the Ouse, and although possibly deprived of its Regency architecture, proudly possessing unrivalled cultural facilities, including a university – a dream that eventually became a reality. A further move towards establishing cultural status for Brighton was the introduction of an annual 'Festival of the Arts', first planned in 1964 when Sir Ian Hunter was appointed Artistic Director. The first Festival was launched in April 1967 and had considerable success and the Festival can now be said to have become a part of the town's life and added something to an already established cosmopolitan reputation. By the late 1960s the full effect of London as a competitor in the field of arts entertainment was being felt; just as it had been so easy to reach Brighton and savour the delights of life at the seaside, so the reverse flow to the capital to enjoy top-class music and drama has meant chronic problems for the viability and success of local promotion of the arts. The struggle to retain the Brighton Philharmonic Orchestra provides a striking example of this. The Theatre Royal, however, has maintained a high standard in staging a distinguished succession of pre-London productions, joined more recently by the excellent facilities available at the Brighton Centre.

The underlying dilemma of expansion versus the necessity of preserving the historic character of Brighton reached a crisis around 1960, when tremendous pressure was exerted in the private sector to abandon planning constraints and again seek a transformation of the traditional appearance of Brighton. In the late 1950s and early 1960s the clearance of the area west of West Street emphasised the need for wise and imaginative planning to be exercised in its future development. In 1960 mounting public concern led the Corporation to confer with Sir High Casson for advice on future planning policy. Among his comments Sir Hugh stated that 'The area round Russell Square and Grenville Place needed particularly sensitive handling ...'[27] but in the event the 'handling' was little short of disastrous. Grenville Place was destroyed and the lasting effect on Russell Square can be seen in illustration no. 156.

As Brighton moved into the 1970s there was a change of attitude towards the problems of conservation, and signs that the rich heritage of later 19th-century buildings in the town also deserved attention. As Pevsner remarked, 'There is Victorian Brighton as well, and this is no less rewarding'. Except for the demolition of the *Old Bedford* in 1965 the main hotels have survived, and one, the *Clarence*, in North Street, carefully converted to alternative use. Attention has been paid to the renewal of housing in central areas. The Frederick Street Development, opened in 1979, indicated a welcome rejection of high-rise policy, and also a more sensitive attitude is evident with 'infilling' – especially well handled recently in Manchester Street and Richmond Place. Yet although the future for the historic identity of Brighton seems in many ways more hopeful, the pressure is still on, and the dilemma still very much alive. On 7 May 1986 the *Evening Argus* devoted a leading article to such difficulties: 'Brighton has a problem ... how to reconcile the gaudy, raucous nature of many tourist attractions with beautiful architecture', going on to hope that the pressure to provide more tourist attractions at Kemp Town and between the Piers would be resolved so as to keep a reasonable balance of principles. Let us hope so; Brighton is beautiful, and its environment and historic identity very precious; something to be cherished and enjoyed by all, now and in the future. Clifford Musgrave writes convincingly why Brighton deserves special treatment: '... there will always be the exhilarating air, the dazzling sunshine, the ever-changing sea and sky – all those elements that go to make up "the brilliancy of Brighton"; something that creates a wonderful sense of well-being and gives the promise of delight – that stimulates the mind to fresh thoughts and ideas; something that has created the idea of Brighton as a pleasure city that is unique on the face of the earth'.

References

1. 'Brighton' derives from the Saxon Beorhthelm's Tun, or Brihthelm's Tun. Numerous variants were in use but the modern form appears in 1660, and was in general use by the latter part of the 18th century.
2. Brighthelmston Lewes – in the Barony of Lewes; Brighthelmston Michelham, belonging to the Augustinian Priory of Michelham, and the paramount manor of Atlingworth, which included St Nicholas.
3. OE Stoney or paved (?) area. Possibly connected with a number of prehistoric Sarsen stones found in the area in 1823 and later used as the base of the Steine fountain.
4. Of what size is problematical. This area may also have been the site for a Saxon church, which also may have been situated in the 'lower town'.
5. Named West Laine, North Laine, Hilly Laine, Little Laine and East Laine, comprising an area of nearly one thousand acres.
6. *De Tabe Glandulari, sui De Usu Aquae Marinae in Morbis Glandulari Dissertatio.* Oxford, 1750, later eds. 1755, 1760 and 1769. A number of unauthorised versions also appeared.
7. Observed by Fanny Burney in her letters of 1780 quoting reports by Mrs. Thrale.
8. The recognition of sunshine as beneficial, and the cult of sun bathing had well over a hundred years to wait before becoming part of the seaside holiday ritual.
9. H. Colvin, *Biographical Dict. of British Architects 1600-1840*, 2nd ed. (1978), p. 349.
10. Another exotic health spot, a Turkish bath, was erected in 1868 in West Street and, like Brill's, became the site of a cinema (Academy, now Academy House) in 1911.
11. *Fashionable Brighton 1820-1860*, p. 14.
12. Bishop, *A Peep into the Past*, p. 139.
13. In 1823 Busby & Wilds plans for a classical-style church on this site were rejected in favour of Charles Barry's Gothick design. The partnership also lost to Barry in designs submitted for the Sussex County Hospital in 1828.
14. *See* Dale & Gray, *Brighton Old and New*, 1976, p. 43.
15. *Journal*, 1851.
16. *Ruskin in Oxford*, 1904.
17. Immortalised in Charles Rossiter's painting *To Brighton and Back for 3s. 6d.* (RA 1859).
18. *Life in Brighton*, p. 271.
19. See plate no. 136.
20. 1851 Census of church attendance.
21. See D. R. Elleray, *The Victorian Churches of Sussex*, pp. 13-21.
22. *The Future of Brighton: what the electric railway means*, 21 Jan, p. xxvi.
23. See Obituary, *Brighton & Hove Herald*, 15 Feb 1941.
24. *The Brighton I should like to see*, in *The Oak* (Brighton & Sussex Building Soc. magazine), February 1935.
25. By Wells W. Coates, F.R.I.B.A., pioneer of the 'modern movement' of the 1930s who helped to form Modern Architectural Research.
26. E. W. Gilbert, *Brighton ...*, pp. 252-3.
27. See H. A. N. Brockman, 'Churchill Square, Brighton', in *Financial Times*, 28 May 1968.

Founding & Early Days

9. During the 16th century there was a constant threat from raids by the French on the southern coast of England, and in 1514 Brighton was sacked and burnt. The event was recorded in this contemporary drawing which gives the only known view of the town's medieval appearance – a square bounded by East, West and North Streets, with St Nicholas to the north-west, and the single street of Hove village to the west.

10. This early view of Brighton in 1784 illustrates the town as shown in the 1778 map – still essentially a town standing by the sea, and not yet looking towards it.

11. Dr. Russell's salt-water cure began at Brighton around 1750. Visitors taking the treatment were in the care of 'dippers' (for ladies) and 'bathers' (for gentlemen). 'Smoaker' Miles was the first of the Brighton bathers to establish a small group of bathing machines. Miles attended the Prince Regent following his arrival in 1783.

12. Martha Gunn (1726-1815), 'venerable Priestess of the Bath' and one of the great characters of early Brighton. She was the leading bathing woman after the arrival of Dr. Russell in the town and 'dipped' many of the notable ladies of the period. She was also a favourite of George IV and received many favours from him. The Gunn family still exists in Brighton and a public house in Upper Lewes road was renamed to commemorate Martha in 1972. Martha's headstone may be seen in St Nicholas's cemetery.

13. Three views illustrating the evolution of the Royal Pavilion during the period 1787-1823. (a) Henry Holland's simple classical-style residence commissioned by the Prince Regent and interestingly incorporating bow fronts. (b) Holland's Marine Pavilion in transition (1818) with the first flanking additions by John Nash, commissioned in 1815 to carry out extensive work. The 'Indian' style was influenced by William Porden's nearby Riding Stables (Dome), erected in 1803. Nash completed the new Pavilion in 1823. (c) The Royal Pavilion much as it appears today, photographed c.1910. One of the best buys ever made by the Borough was its acquisition in 1850 for £50,000.

14. (*above*) John Nash's drawing of the Pavilion Banqueting Room, 1824. Towards the end of the 19th century, and especially following the establishment of the Regency Exhibition, this room was fully refurnished and now provides a splendid climax for the many visitors to the Royal Pavilion.

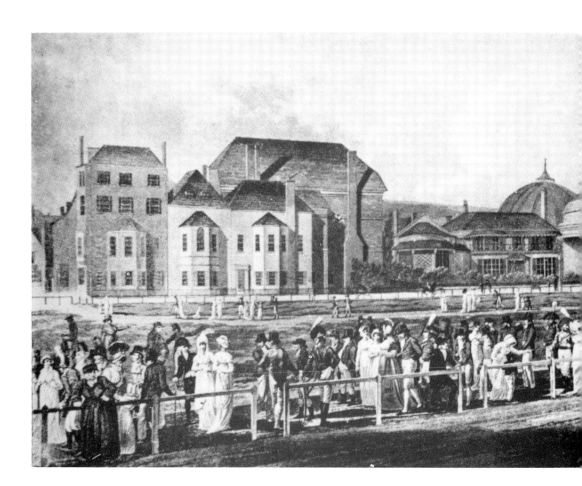

15. (*above*) The Royal Pavilion North Gate in about 1910. First called the North Lodge, it was erected in 1832 by Joseph Good at the direction of William IV, using Nash's original designs. Its Portland and Bath stone construction give it the most durable fabric of the whole Pavilion group.

16. (*left*) View of the Pavilion and Steine with the Promenade, from a print of 1806, buildings by Cracklow and figures by William M. Craig. The Prince Regent (mounted) is on the right with his aide Sir Benjamin Bloomfield, and on the extreme left is Martha Gunn. Of all the early views of Brighton, this best illustrates the Steine as the fashionable centre of the town's social life.

E. View of the Royal Pavilion. Brighton.

S. View of the Royal Stables. Brighton.

N. Elevation of the Royal Stables. Brighton.

17.   Three views of the Royal Pavilion and Stables c.1830 by James Rouse. The
north aspect of Porden's Stables (Dome) shows the original facade before the
remodelling carried out in 1902 (for the enlargement of the Museum and
Library) which altered the original Church Street frontage designed by J. H.
Good after his appointment as Pavilion architect in 1822.

18. (*above*) Mahomed's Indian Baths were opened in 1786 on the site now occupied by the *Queen's Hotel*, where a plaque records Sake Deen Mahomed's many famous 'cures'.

MADDOCKS SC

S. D. Mahomed,
Shampooing Surgeon,
BRIGHTON.

19. (*right*) Sake Deen Mahomed (1749-1851) was born at Patna, married an Irish girl, and became famous in Brighton when he opened a vapour bath in 1786. In 1822 he was appointed 'Shampooing Surgeon to His Majesty King George IV' and was placed in charge of the Pavilion bathroom. His son Arthur Akhbar Mahomed continued the baths into the 1870s.

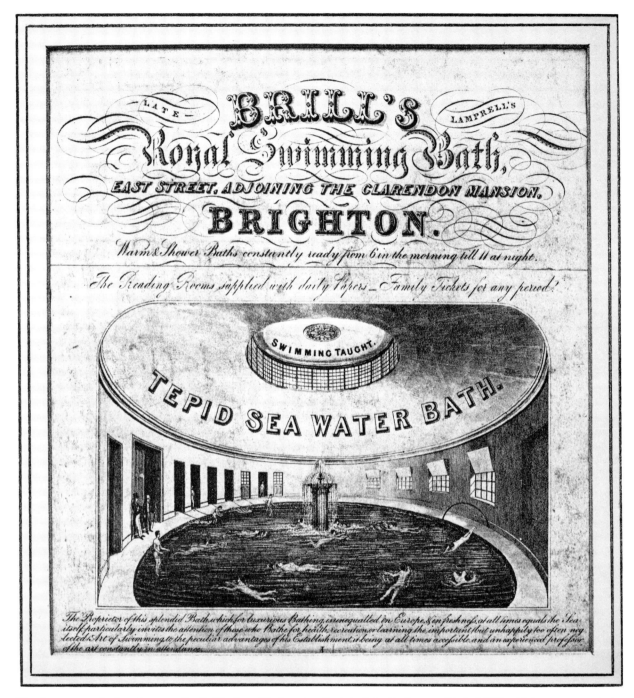

20. An engraved advertisement for Brill's Royal Swimming Bath (originally Lamprell's in 1823) which once occupied a circular building, known locally as the 'bunion', at the south-east end of East Street. The 'bunion' was demolished in 1869 when larger baths were erected on the north side, these in turn being swept away for the Savoy cinema development in 1929.

The German Spa Queens Park Brighton.

Pub. by C. Andrews 11 St James's St 1841

21. The Royal German Spa, Queen's Park, was erected by Dr. F. A. Struve of Dresden in 1825, and designed by a Mr. Loraine. The Spa catered for the fashionable demand for mineral waters and produced a range of imitation fluids in the style of Ems, Seltzer, Kesselbrunnen etc. Royal patronage was granted and the Pump Room enjoyed visits from William IV and other royal personages. The Spa continued as a Pump Room until c.1875, and later became Hooper Struve Ltd., mineral water manufacturers, which closed in 1960.

22. The Royal German Spa, Queen's Park, as it is today – a remarkable example of conservation by surgery! After neglect and vandalism, Lord Holford saved the Spa from demolition in 1967, but some years passed before any action was taken.

23.   The Royal Circus was opened by Kendall & Co. in 1808 at the bottom of Carlton Hill, the site being commemorated by the present Circus Street. Although providing numerous facilities and amusements in addition to the circus, the building did not succeed and, after becoming a bazaar and later an art gallery, it was demolished in the 1830s.

24.   Ireland's Pleasure Gardens were opened in 1822 in an attempt to repeat the success of the former Promenade Grove in New Road. An extraordinary range of attractions were provided – refreshments, cricket, Gothic buildings, a grotto, maze and frequent firework displays. But after three years the venture failed, Ireland lost his money and turned to innkeeping, the Gardens being cleared for the erection of Park Crescent in 1829.

Ireland's Royal Grounds

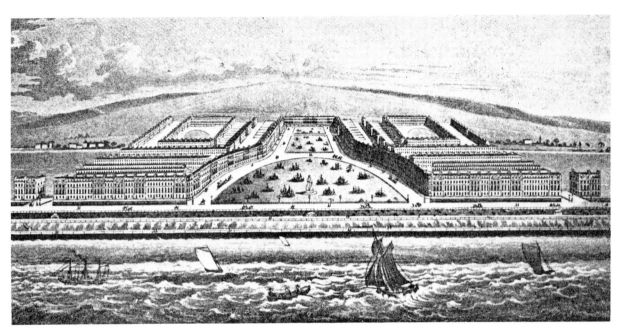

25. Brighton's greatest *tour de force* of Regency architecture is Kemp Town, a Nash-inspired estate of the grandest dimensions, the spans of Sussex Square and Lewes Crescent being 300 and 840 feet, considerably larger than Bath's Royal Crescent. Developed by Thomas R. Kemp in 1823-c.1845, the building was mainly by Thomas Cubitt, the design by Busby and Wilds, and the Esplanade and slopes by H. E. Kendall, jnr. Kemp occupied No. 22 Sussex Square in 1827, and Cubitt lived at 13 Lewes Crescent c.1846-55.

26. Close-up view of the Chain Pier head in 1833, which for several years became a fashionable meeting place. The area was paved with 200 tons of Purbeck stone and was provided with a sundial and telescope. The bell beneath the southernmost tower signalled the departure of packet boats.

27. (*above*) One of the great sights of 19th-century Brighton was the Suspension Chain Pier, built in 1823 from the highly original designs of Captain Samuel Brown at a cost of £27,000. The grand opening on 25 November was attended by 250 guests of 'rank and respectability' including Thomas R. Kemp, Dr. Gibney and the Portuguese Ambassador. This photograph c.1890 shows Volk's Electric Railway passing beneath the land end. Some six years later on 4 December 1896 the pier was destroyed by a violent storm.

Brighton Royal Suspension Pier.

ANNUAL TICKET.

1850.

Palace.

28. (*left*) Royal Ticket for Brighton Suspension Pier, 1850.

29. (*right*) William IV succeeded to the throne in 1830 and soon arrived in Brighton to renew the royal connections of George IV. The new monarch continued his brother's love of both Brighton and the Pavilion and supervised the erection of the North Gateway with Nash. Especially admirable was William's generosity towards the ageing Mrs. Fitzherbert.

30. (*left*) Queen Adelaide, consort of William IV, became a popular and well-loved figure in Brighton. She attended St George's Kemp Town as her 'Chapel Royal' and her gifts of plate are still preserved at the church. Both Queen's Park and Adelaide Crescent were named after her. This portrait was published in August 1830, 'expressly for Bells Weekly Messenger'.

Churches

31. The parish church of St Nicholas dates from the 14th century but was restored by R. C. Carpenter in 1853. There is a fine 15th-century screen, and the font (c.1100, from an earlier church) has carvings depicting Biblical subjects and scenes from the life of St Nicholas. There are monuments to Thomas Read Kemp, Wellington and Dr. Johnson, and a tomb by Westmacott for his wife who died in Brighton in 1834.

32. St Margaret's, Cannon Place, was Brighton's finest classical-style church, destroyed in 1959 in preparation for the Sussex Heights development. The church was designed by Isaac Clarke in 1824 as an adjunct to the new Regency Square. In the 1870s a chancel was added, to the designs of J. Oldrid Scott.

33. (*above*) St Peter's, built during 1824-28 as a new parish church, one of the first examples of a Gothic revival church in England, was designed by Sir Charles Barry. St Peter's was enlarged in 1906. Round Hill tower mill can be seen in the distance.

34. (*right*) The Rev. Henry Venn Elliott (d.1865) was Perpetual Curate of St Mary's Chapel Rock Gardens which had been founded by his father Charles in 1827. Nine years later he opened St Mary's Hall Girls' School (by George Basevi), Kemp Town, adding St Mark's as the school chapel in 1849.

STBARTSPAROCHIALOUTING.

35. A fine array of Edwardian millinery at St Bartholomew's parochial outing in 1910. On the right is the *Mezeppa Inn* which stood at the top of Ann Street (corner of New York Street).

36. (*left*) The towering red brick St Bartholomew's, Ann Street, was built by Father A. D. Wagner in 1872-74 and is the crowning glory of Brighton's Victorian churches – in Pevsner's words, 'an unforgettable experience'. The nave, internally buttressed with side chapels, is 135 feet high, and there is Art Nouveau furnishing (1895-1910) by Henry Wilson.

37. (*below*) All Saints' Eaton Road, Hove, designed by J. L. Pearson, is one of the great achievements of the 19th-century Gothic Revival. The church was founded by Canon Thomas Peacey. Building began in 1889 on a site given by Mrs. Benett Stanford, and the nave and aisles were consecrated on 1 May 1891, the chancel being completed ten years later when All Saints' became Hove parish church.

38. (*above left*) A portrait of the Rev. A. D. Wagner, Vicar of St Paul's, West Street. During the latter half of the 19th century Wagner devoted a large fortune, and all his energy, to promoting the High Church cause in Brighton, and providing houses for the poor.

39. (*above right*) An informal photograph of the Rev. James Vaughan and his wife in old age. Vaughan spent 41 years at Christ Church, Montpelier Road, and during this time gained a high reputation as one of the most able preachers in Victorian Brighton. He published several volumes of sermons.

40. (*right*) During the Victorian period Brighton became known for its preachers and perhaps the most notable and sensational was the Reverend F. W. Robertson whose brief ministry at Holy Trinity, Ship Street, 1847 to 1853, made the church a household word and drew vast and fashionable crowds from a wide area on Sundays. Robertson died at the early age of 37, and was described by Dickens as one of the greatest masters of elocution.

41. (*left*) The importance of the Jewish community in Brighton and Hove's history is symbolised by the Middle Street Synagogue. The foundation stone was laid by Louis Cohen in 1874 and the interior of the building is rich in traditional furnishings and colourful decoration.

42. (*below*) The end of another of Brighton's Victorian churches – St Anne's, Burlington Street, being demolished in April 1986. Designed in 1863 by Benjamin Ferrey, the interior was notable for its unusual carvings of ferns and flowers, some of which have fortunately been saved. It is regrettable that some alternative public use could not have been found for this attractive building.

Schools

43. (*right*) The former Gothic National School, Church Street (opposite New Road), demolished in 1971. The school was erected in 1829 and designed by Stroud and Mew with later additions by Cheeseman. It formed one of a small number of buildings in this style in Brighton, which makes its loss particularly regrettable.

44. (*below*) The former Diocesan Training College for Schoolmistresses, Ditchling Road, is an important example of early Victorian gothic architecture employing local flint. The College was founded in 1854 and closed in 1939, and since the war has been occupied by the Royal Engineers' Record Office.

45.   Pupils and staff at the Middle Street School in 1895. Founded as the Union School in 1805 with funds provided by Edward Goff, it was enlarged in 1875-6 and completely re-built in modern style in the early 1970s.

46.   Roedean School forming a background to the Black Rock-Shoreham air race in May 1911. The school celebrated its centenary in 1985 and was founded by the sisters Penelope, Dorothy and Millicent Lawrence in a house in Lewes Crescent. In 1897 work began on the present school from designs by Sir John W. Simpson. During the Second World War Roedean was occupied by the Royal Navy and named H.M.S. *Vernon*.

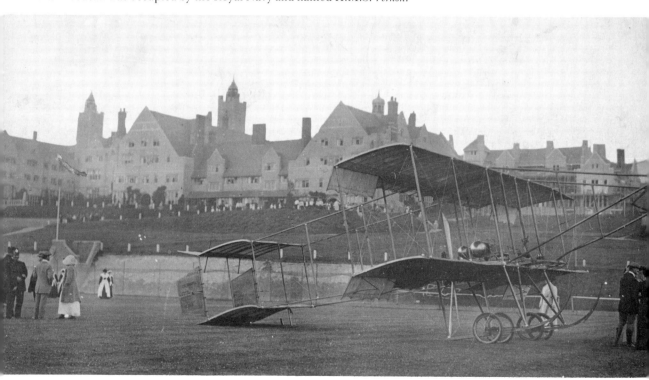

47. Brighton College, founded in 1845, first occupied No. 13 Portland Place, later moving to its present site in March 1848 where the first buildings were designed by Gilbert Scott. The foundation stone was laid by the Bishop of Chichester in June 1848. Major extensions in 1885-7 were by an old boy, T. G. Jackson, but the elaborate gateway tower was never completed.

48. The Temple, Montpelier Road, now housing the Brighton and Hove Girls'
High School, founded in 1880. The name 'Temple' is said to derive from its
proportions being similar to Solomon's temple. The school retains the original
cobble flint boundary walls. The Temple was designed in 1819 by Amon Wilds
for Thomas Read Kemp who occupied the house until he moved to No.22
Sussex Square in 1827.

49. First World War wounded being accommodated at Brighton and Hove Grammar School, Dyke Road, in September
1914. The school was founded in 1859 in Grand Parade and the present building was designed by S. B. Russell in 1912.

50. A stage coach about to leave the *Old Ship Hotel*. The hotel is Brighton's oldest inn and became the assembly rooms of the new resort, the original terminus for coaches, and venue for town commissioners' meetings.

51. The famous coachman Edwin Fownes (1851-1943) outside the *Metropole* in 1899. The primrose and black coach 'Nimrod' claimed to be the best turned out and fastest on the road. Fownes retired and became landlord of the *Avon Hotel* in Amesbury in 1916, later dying at the advanced age of 92. Note the ornate glass and iron hotel porch removed in 1964 when the *Metropole* was 'improved'.

52. The historic opening of the Shoreham branch of the London and Brighton Railway on 11 May 1840 in the presence of Sir John Rennie. The first train left at 3 p.m. to the strains of the national anthem. It carried a select company of 230 passengers and took 12 minutes to reach Shoreham. In the evening the Directors gave a splendid dinner at the *Old Ship*. At first six trains in each direction provided the weekday service, with five on Sundays.

Published by W. Grant News Agent 5 Castle Square.

View of the Railway Terminus Brighton

53. Brighton Railway Station in about 1850 showing the remarkable embanked site chosen by John Rennie and the steep descent of Trafalgar Street towards St Peter's church. The design by David Mocatta in an Italianate style cost £12,000. The elegant facade is now obscured by canopies.

54. The Brighton Locomotive Works c.1870, showing the extensive running sheds. The Works were served by three distinguished railway engineers during the 19th century – John C. Craven appointed Superintendent in 1847, followed by Stroudley, and then R. J. Billinton, 1890-1904. All designed notable locomotives and in 1896 some 12 engines were being built yearly. The Works slowly declined after electrification and closed in 1964.

55. (*left*) William Stroudley (1833-1889) became Locomotive Superintendent at Brighton Railway Works in 1869 and was responsible for expanding them in 1871. Stroudley was an outstanding locomotive designer creating the famous 0-6-0 'Terrier' tank engines and the express 'Gladstone' class. The Brighton Works were established in 1852 and had an important effect upon the economic and social life of the town.

56. (*below*) The Brighton Viaduct, a superb example of early railway engineering designed by Sir John Rennie, was completed in March 1846 after ten months' work. It is 400 yards long, up to 67 feet high and has 27 arches. In May 1943 a German bomber scored a direct hit on the central arch but the gap was soon bridged.

57. A D2 Class and other locomotives in Brighton station c.1904. The station's iron and glass canopy is a splendid example of railway architecture designed in 1883 by H. E. Wallis, the iron cast by John Every of Lewes. Plans to redevelop the station in 1974 were fortunately rejected.

58. The prestigious *Southern Belle* Pullman Express began running between London and Brighton on 1 November 1908. The journey (twice daily) took one hour and a first class *annual* ticket cost £33. The train greatly enhanced Brighton as the leading holiday resort.

BRIGHTON
IN 60 MINUTES

BY

"The Southern Belle,"

- Week-Days and Sundays. -

	WEEKDAYS.		SUNDAYS and XMAS DAY.	
	A·M.	P.M	A.M	P.M
VICTORIA...... dep.	11 0	3 10	11 0	6 30
	NOON		NOON	
BRIGHTON...... arr.	12 0	4 10	12 0	7 30
	P.M.	P.M.	P.M.	P.M.
BRIGHTON...... dep.	12 20	5 45	5 0	9 30
VICTORIA ...... arr.	1 20	6 45	6 0	10 30

Third-Class Pullman Cars
ARE RUN IN THIS TRAIN ON WEEK-DAYS.

LUNCHEONS, TEAS AND SUPPERS ARE OBTAINABLE on the Cars at Short Notice and at a Moderate Charge.

(These Arrangements are subject to Alteration).

Fast Business Trains
WITH PULLMAN CARS ATTACHED,
are run between London and Brighton—morning & evening.

SPECIAL ANNUAL TICKETS.
Between London and Brighton

1st Class £33.   3rd Class £24.

3 and 6 Monthly Tickets pro rata.

For full particulars apply at Brighton Station or to Superintendent of the Line, London Bridge.

WILLIAM FORBES, GENERAL MANAGER.

59. The last steam-hauled *Southern Belle* ran on 31 December 1932, and was then replaced by five-car all-Pullman electric trains. These, running every hour, were renamed *Brighton Belle* on 1 June 1934. The withdrawal of this famous train on 30 April 1972 must amount to one of the most unfortunate decisions ever made by British Rail.

60. The Dyke Railway opened on 1 September 1887 and continued until increasing competition from the motor car led to its closure on 31 December 1938. The standard gauge track reached a level of 501 feet near Round Hill. Between 1933 and 1937 a steam 'Sentinel' railbus made at the Wagon Works, Shrewsbury, by Metropolitan Cammell was in regular service.

61. Magnus Volk opened his electric railway in 1883 and in November 1896 an extension was built running from the Banjo Groyne to Rottingdean. It was styled the Brighton and Rottingdean Seashore Electric Railway but soon became known as 'Daddy-long-legs'. The extraordinary contraption actually ran on sea-bed track, but persistent blocking by sand and shingle led to its abandonment in 1901. The double-decker cars carried up to 150 passengers and flew the red ensign when at sea!

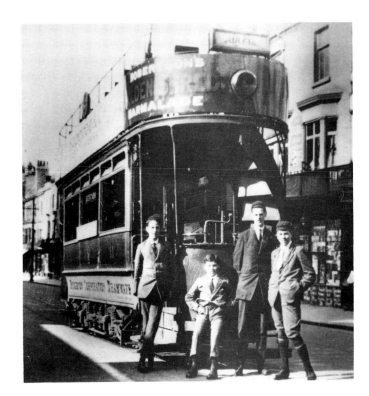

62. A Brighton A Class tram in Queen's Road c.1914. The tramway opened on 25 November 1901 with 30 open-top cars made by British Westinghouse. The livery was cream/maroon/brown and the system, under the direction of William March, proved one of the most efficient in Britain. By the mid 1930s the 9½-mile system was carrying 24 million passengers per year.

63. The famous Volk's Electric
Railway was opened in August
1883 by Magnus Volk, son of a
German clock-maker. For many
years the section just east of the
Banjo Groyne formed a bridge
over the beach – an exciting
stretch for travellers at high tide
in rough weather!

64. This Milnes-Daimler 20 h.p. motor bus was the first to be licensed by Brighton, Hove & Preston United Omnibus Co. and began working on Christmas Eve 1903. This photograph was taken opposite Steine Lane some days later, in January 1904.

65. Motor racing on the mile-long Madeira Drive was promoted by Harry Preston in 1905 in the face of opposition from the council. The photograph shows the first Motor Race Week in August that year when entrants included such famous names as Theodore Schneider, C. S. Rolls and Clifford Earp. The racing was to become a popular annual event.

66. The *Brighton Queen* (603 tons) was one of several pleasure steamers which were once such an attractive part of holidays in Brighton. Built in 1897 on the Clyde, she was later purchased from the Brighton, Worthing & South Coast Steamboat Co. and rebuilt by P. & A. Campbell Ltd., only to be lost minesweeping during the 1914-18 War.

67. During May-August 1939 both trams and trolley-buses were running in Brighton – the former being withdrawn on 31 August, and the latter introduced on 1 May. Shown here are the F Class tram no. 68, and the AEC 661T trolley-bus no. 36, at the Steine terminus. Trolley-bus services continued for 22 years until 30 June 1961.

Beside the Seaside

DON'T BE FRIGHTENED, DEAR!
(IT'S ONLY A LITTLE SWELL FROM THE PIER.)

68. In 1848 a series of satirical lithographs published by 'Alfred Crowquill' (Alfred Forrester) portrayed the 'new visitors' to Brighton, that is, the middle-class holiday-maker and tripper. The one illustrated here indicates that the age of the 'ogler' was by no means over, even by 1848.

69. Brighton beach looking towards the Palace Pier in about 1907. Notice the great number of fishing and other craft, bathing machines, and a horse working one of the capstans on the left.

70. The Fish Market at the bottom of East Street was once a busy and interesting place and always attracted a crowd of onlookers. Following the Second World War complaints were made concerning the hygiene of the market, and eventually, in spite of strong opposition, it was closed and moved to new premises.

71.   Fishing boats and bathing machines at the bottom of West Street in 1890. Beyond is the West Pier before the enlargement and erection of the South Pavilion in 1894. Note the 'Watermens Regatta' placard and the goat-cart in the foreground.

72.   The Aquarium, designed by Eusebius Birch, was opened on 10 August 1872. Apart from its scientific interest, the Aquarium became an important entertainment centre, and was reconstructed in 1929-31 by David Edwards, Borough Surveyor. The Aquarium's popularity has benefited considerably since the introduction of a 'dolphinarium' in 1967.

BRIGHTON AQUARIUMISMS,

SOCIAL AND SCIENTIFIC.

73.   A contemporary satirical cartoon on Brighton's new Aquarium commenting on both inmates and visitors, published in January 1873.

74.   A postcard view from Brighton into Hove c.1925 across the sunken gardens showing the peace monument and the elegant Regency facades of Brunswick Town overlooking the lawns.

75.   The beach at the Brighton-Hove border. Just visible is the 1884 Birdcage Bandstand and the continental-style *Norfolk Hotel*, rebuilt by Horatio Goulty in 1865 and nearly lost in the A. V. Poster redevelopment plans of 1964.

76. Traditional seaside holidays, with plenty more for the Skylarks! For many years three of these popular 'schooner yachts' were owned by Captain Collins, two being lost at the Dunkirk evacuation in 1940.

77. The Brunswick Lawns in 1910. The Lawns became a highly fashionable rendezvous, especially on Sundays, during the latter part of the 19th century – a later equivalent of the Steine of Regency times.

78. Brighton beach thronged with children in the mid 1890s. In the distance the old Chain Pier and above part of the new Palace Pier under construction.

79. The West Pier may claim to be the most elegant pier in existence – a fact that makes its disastrous neglect since the 1939-45 War hard to understand. The pier was designed by Eusebius Birch in 1864-66 and the splendid South Pavilion added in 1894. It is to be hoped that the West Pier will eventually be restored to its former glory.

80. A photograph of the South Pavilion Theatre just after its opening on the Palace Pier in 1901. The theatre was later remodelled and became a popular place of entertainment. In 1986 the building was demolished with the intention of re-erecting it at a later date.

Leisure, Pleasure & Sport

81. *(left)* Frederick William Lillywhite (1792-1854), the famous 'Nonpareil Bowler', a bricklayer from West Hampnett, moved to Brighton in 1822 and later to Hove. In 1837 he took over the *Royal Sovereign Inn*, Preston Street, which then had an adjoining cricket ground.

82. *(right)* John Wisden (1826-1884) was born in Brighton and played for Sussex from 1845 to 1863, taking 344 wickets during his career. In 1864 he first published the *Cricketers' Almanack* costing one shilling, a price unchanged until 1915.

83. Drummond and Basebe's celebrated subscription drawing of a cricket match between Sussex and Kent at Ireland's old ground north of St Peter's in 1849. Among the 66 portraits are Fuller Piltch (taking strike) and William Lillywhite, bowling.

84. The Sussex county cricket team in 1908. The first County matches were played at Ireland's Gardens, now the site of Park Crescent, but then moved to the Brunswick Ground, Hove, in 1848 and later to the present County Ground in 1872.

E. PANNELL
Photo

A. NELMES.   G. WHITING.   J. ROBSON.   W. CRINSON.   J. BUTT.

J. McGHIE.   G. WHITTINGTON. J. LUMLEY. R. ROUTLEDGE. F. BLACKMAN. H. MIDDLETON. W. BOOTH. E.H. ELLIOTT.

R. ARMSTRONG. G. FEATHERSTONE. W. CONNOR. R.E. LONGSTAFFE. J. LEEMING. C.G. WEBB. W.H. JONES. W. HASTINGS. H. LONGSTAFFE.

J.H. EACOCK.   J. COLMAN.   R. CRAIG.   J. HAWORTH.

85. The Albion football team in 1909-10. The first professional team, Brighton United, was founded in 1898 using the County Cricket ground at Hove. This club failed in 1900, and was succeeded by the Brighton & Hove Rangers which existed for two years before the Brighton and Hove Albion was founded in 1902.

86. Brighton's first permanent theatre opened in 1774 in North Street. It was superseded in 1790 by the Duke Street theatre, constructed mainly of wood, with an elegant interior including a royal box. In 1794 it was acquired by Hewitt Cobb who transferred the licence to his new theatre in New Road in 1807.

87. (*above*) The Theatre Royal, New Road, was opened in June 1807 by Hewitt Cobb and John Brunton with Charles Kemble and his wife performing in *Hamlet*. The theatre soon became a pre-eminent provincial house and many great actors appeared there including Mrs. Siddons, Edmund and Charles Kean, Grimaldi and Mme. Vestris.

Under the Patronage of His Royal Highness

THE PRINCE REGENT.

Theatre Royal, Brighton.

On FRIDAY, August the 30th 1816,

Will be presented, the most favorite, and popular production of the late R.B SHERIDAN, Esq. called

The RIVALS;

Or, a Trip to Bath.

Bob Acres, by Mr. HARLEY.
Sir Anthony Absolute, Mr. BUTLER.   Captain Absolute, Mr. STANLEY.
Sir Lucius O'Trigger, Mr. CORY.   Faulkland, Mr. VINING.
Fag, Mr. ALFORD.   Coachman, Mr. COATES.
David, by Mr. KNIGHT.
Julia Melville, Miss NORTON.
Mrs. Malaprop, Mrs. CORY.   Lucy, Mrs. JEFFRIES.
Lydia Languish, by a YOUNG LADY,
Her First Appearance on any Stage.

End of the Play,

A PAS SEUL, by Mr. ALBIN.

In the course of the Evening the following Comic Songs:—

The Pleasures of Brighton. or Love, Liberty, & Salt-water,
By Mr. HARLEY.

And, When I went for a Soldier. by Love I was Twisted,
By Mr. KNIGHT.

To conclude with the Farce of the

Boarding House;

Or Five Hours at Brighton.

Peter Fidget, by Mr. HARLEY.
Admiral Culpepper, Mr. BUTLER.   Alderman Lontract, Mr. WHARTON.
Simon Spatterdash, (a Local Militiaman,) by Mr. KNIGHT.
Caroline Wheatsheaf, Miss JOHANNOT.   Caroline Heartly, Miss BURRELL.
Fanny, Miss HALFORD.   Bridget, Mrs. JEFFRIES.

Boxes 3s.—Pit 2s. 6d.—Gallery, 1s.——Second Price to the Boxes 3s. 6d.—to the Pit, 1s. 6d. to commence at a quarter past Nine o'Clock.
Doors to be opened at a Quarter past Six, and begin at a Quarter past Seven o'clock.

Fleet, Printer, Brighton.

88. (*left*) Playbill for *The Rivals* produced at the Theatre Royal in August 1816 under the patronage of the Prince Regent. Sheridan had died on 7 July the same year.

89. Henry and Nellie Nye Chart, two great names in the theatrical history of Brighton. In 1854 Mr Chart leased the Theatre Royal and inaugurated 40 years of success and stability in its management. On Henry's death in 1875, his wife continued alone with undiminished energy and her work of encouraging visits from top London companies laid the foundation for the great reputation of the Theatre Royal in this century.

LATE MR. H. NYE CHART
(Former Proprietor of Theatre Royal, Brighton).

LATE MRS. NELLIE CHART.

90. Programme cover of the Theatre Royal c.1900 showing the remodelling carried out by the Brighton architect G. E. Clayton in 1894. The roof line was spoilt in 1921 when dormers were installed.

91. (*right*) The North Road Hippodrome was opened in 1891 by the famous circus proprietor Fred Ginnett, and remodelled in 1894 as the Eden Theatre. It became notorious for lurid melodrama, and in 1905 became the Grand. During 1931-40 the theatre was used as a cinema, but reverted to variety thereafter until its closure in 1955. The Grand was burned down in 1965.

92. (*left*) The distinctive family tomb of the Ginnetts in Brighton Extra-Mural Cemetery. Jean-Pierre Ginnett (from Marseilles) established a circus in Southend and in 1876 his son Fred built 'Ginnett's Royal Hippodrome' in Park Crescent Place, later called the Gaiety. The Gaiety closed in 1900 and housed Fryco's factory until its demolition in 1930. In 1891 another Hippodrome (later the Grand) opened in North Road (see plate 91).

93. (*above left*) Max Miller (Thomas H. Sargent, 1895-1963) was born in Brighton and became one of the last great comedians of the British music-hall, the embodiment of the cockney 'cheeky chappie'. Miller joined Jack Sheppard's Entertainers on the West Pier in 1919, appeared frequently at the Hippodrome during the period 1940-1955, and performed at the Royal Variety Show in 1931, 1937 and 1950. His house in Burlington Street bears a commemorative plaque.

94. (*above right*) Brighton's oldest surviving cinema, the Duke of York, Preston Circus, photographed in 1981. It was opened in 1910 on the site of Longhurst's Brewery, and was designed by Clayton & Black.

95. The Regent, Queen's Road, in about 1922, before the completion of the famous roof-top ballroom. A few fragments of the fine terracotta panels on the facade are now preserved in Brighton Museum. The interior of the Regent was among the finest in the world.

96. Good business at the Haddington Street Empire, Hove, during the First World War. The cinema was opened in 1910 by Eddie Scriven in the converted Blatchington Hall and continued until 1933 when competition from the new Lido and Granada forced its closure.

97. The Devil's Dyke, famous for its views. The Suspension Railway seen here operated during the years 1894-1907 during the proprietorship of J. H. Hubbard who also opened the Dyke Railway in 1887 and added much to the amenities of the area.

The Chevalier.

98. (*above*) Wilhelm Kuhe (1823-1912), Czech musician and composer, settled in England in 1847 and became important in Brighton's musical life. In 1871-82 he promoted a successful series of festivals at the West Street Concert Hall and then at the Dome auditorium.

99. (*right*) The flamboyant conductor of the Municipal Orchestra between 1914 and 1924, Henry Lyell-Taylor, had many fans at his West Pier concerts where he introduced the young Isolda Menges.

100. Yehudi Menuhin (left) in conversation with Herbert Menges outside the Dome during the 1968 Brighton Festival. Herbert Menges O.B.E. (b.1902) first appeared as a violinist aged four at Hove, and later studied with Holst and Vaughan Williams. In 1925 he founded the Brighton Symphonic Players, later the Brighton Philharmonic. In 1941 he became joint conductor of the Sadler's Wells Orchestra and continued to conduct in Brighton until his death in 1972.

Buildings & Streets

101. Marlborough House, Old Steine, replaced the original house of that name built in 1769 and later owned by the 4th Duke of Marlborough. In 1786 it was remodelled by W. G. Hamilton, M.P., to the designs of Robert Adam, and may claim to be Brighton's most important house. On the right is Steine House, designed by William Porden in 1804 for Mrs. Fitzherbert who lived there until 1837. The facade was remodelled in 1884 when the Y.M.C.A. occupied the building.

102. The Royal Sussex County Hospital was established by the generosity of the Earl of Egremont and Thomas Read Kemp, the former laying the foundation stone in March 1826. The building (here already extended) was designed by Sir Charles Barry and originally provided for 80 patients. On the right is St George's Chapel, designed by Busby in 1824 to serve the Kemp Town Estate, and frequently used by Queen Adelaide.

103. (*left*) North Gate House, the last survivor of the old Marlborough Row. As No. 8, it was occupied by Lady Conyngham in the early years of the 19th century and later by William IV's private secretary Major-General Sir Herbert Taylor. The oriental-style remodelling carried out in 1832 makes the house one of Brighton's most charming examples of the Regency style.

104. (*right*) The Brighton Art Gallery in about 1910. The Gallery opened in 1873 and was part of the former Stables remodelled by P. C. Lockwood in 1869 for a public Museum and Library. On the left can be seen Lawrence's portrait of the Prince Regent and the end balcony is now part of the Museum restaurant. After housing the permanent collection for many years the Gallery now displays an important collection of Art Nouveau and Deco furniture and ornaments.

105. (*left*) No. 1 Lewes Crescent (now Fife House) and No. 14 Chichester Terrace (amalgamated and separated some three times) are perhaps the most famous houses in Brighton. The ownership of the 6th Duke of Devonshire, resident 1829-58, led to many distinguished visitors including William IV, Princess Lieven, Metternich and Lord Lytton, while later ownership by the Duke and Duchess of Fife brought the Duchess's father Edward VII, the Princess Royal and King Haakon of Norway.

106. Wykeham Terrace, adjacent to St Nicholas, is the only example of Regency Gothic left in Brighton (apart from a fragment of Gothic House, later Plummer's, now Debenham's, in Western Road). The Terrace has now been largely refurbished, and the attractive central tower feature suggests the work of either A. H. Wilds or Mew.

107. Belvedere, Montpelier Road, a pleasant Tudor-style Victorian house, was built c.1840 by Mary Ann Wagner who left it to her nephew Arthur D. Wagner in 1868. Father Wagner spent his last years at Belvedere and died there in January 1902. Later the house was a school, and in 1933 became the *Park Royal Hotel* until it was demolished in 1975 and replaced by the Park Royal flats.

Published by W.H.Mason, Repository of Arts, King's Road, Brighton.

Belvedere, Montpelier Road.

108. (*left*) Attree Villa, Queen's Park, in c.1890. This fine Italianate house was originally the home of Thomas Attree, Clerk to the Brighton Commissioners, 1810-1823, and was designed by Sir Charles Barry. From 1909 to 1967 it was occupied by the Roman Catholic Xaverian College, but later became sadly neglected. In spite of being a listed building, Brighton Council allowed it to be demolished in 1972. The once beautiful site is now disfigured by mediocre development.

109. (*right*) The old *King and Queen*, Marlborough Place, a little before demolition in 1933. The inn was originally part of a farm c.1700, and served as Brighton's corn market until 1868. The inn's name refers to George III and Queen Charlotte.

110. (*above*) An Edwardian view of Regency Square. The Square, once known as Belle Vue Field, was owned by Joshua Flesher Hanson who developed the area in 1818, possibly employing Amon Wilds as architect. The estate was completed by 1828 and included Cannon Place, the *Regency Inn*, St Margaret's and Russell Square. To the left is the Royal Sussex Regiment South African War Memorial and, to the right, the original corner building replaced by a modern block in the 1960s. An underground car park was also constructed in the Square at this time.

111. (*right*) In 1833 Amon Henry Wilds designed for himself a small oriental residence in Western Place known as the Western Pavilion because of its similarity to Nash's Royal Pavilion. This delightful building has recently been carefully restored.

112. (*above*) The 'other Brighton' –
Carlton Row slums before
demolition in 1933. From 1840 the
area around Carlton Hill and Sussex
Street became notorious for its
poverty, disease and drunkenness,
and in 1882 an attack on the
deplorable health conditions at
Brighton in the *Lancet* did great
harm to the town's reputation.

113. (*left*) The Blind School in
Eastern Road was designed by the
local architect Somers Clarke in
1865, and its remarkable Venetian
Gothic style made it one of the most
important Victorian buildings in
Brighton. Plans for the expansion of
the County Hospital led to its
demolition in 1958.

114. (*right*) West Street in about 1905 showing St Paul's dominating the area with its unique timber lantern tower – the first symbol of the Anglican revival in Brighton, designed by R. C. Carpenter in 1848.

115. (*below*) The same view of West Street in 1985 illustrating the replacement of traditional stone by heartless concrete: the now derelict Odeon (1937) abutting St Paul's, and the 'deplorable Top Rank building' (Dale), erected in 1966, which may be said to be the most brash contribution so far to Brighton's sea front.

116. The Clock Tower in about 1910 with a L.B. & S.C.R. horse-drawn van in the foreground. The baroque/classical-style tower, designed by John Johnson at a cost of £2,000, commemorates Queen Victoria's Golden Jubilee (1887) and was given by a local advertising contractor, John Willing.

117. Crowded late-Victorian scene on the King's Road dominated by Alfred Waterhouse's massive terracotta *Metropole Hotel* erected in 1890. The best feature of the hotel was an elegant roof with distinctive green spire, barbarously ripped off during 'improvements' in the early 1960s.

118. (*above*) Preston Manor, now the
Thomas-Stanford Museum, dates from
1739 and replaced an earlier mansion
owned by the Shirleys. It later belonged
to the Western family and then to the
Stanfords. In 1932 the house and
contents were left to the town by Sir
Charles and Lady Thomas-Stanford.

119. (*right*) A photograph of Pool
Valley in about 1900, showing one of
Brighton's most famous buildings –
Cowley's Bunn Shoppe, erected in
1794, and owned by the Cowley family
until c.1940. The original mathematical
tiles are well preserved but the shop
front has been altered. On the left is the
site of Brill's Baths.

120. (*left*) The Lanes, perhaps the most characteristic part of old Brighton, photographed in about 1914. Although no building dates from before c.1700, the area has both medieval scale and configuration and is a great tourist attraction, especially because of its many antique shops.

121. (*below*) The old *Bedford Hotel* was designed by a local architect, Thomas Cooper, in 1829 and was patronised by many famous visitors, including Charles Dickens. In 1965 fire seriously damaged the hotel and, although restoration was possible, it was unfortunately replaced by the new *Bedford Hotel* – completely out of scale and sympathy with much of the sea front.

122. (*right*) No. 90 Montpelier Road, Grosvenor House (once a school), is a delightful late-Regency villa made unique by the addition of a superb Art Nouveau iron porch, complete with spiky florets and distinctive coloured leaded glass.

123. (*below*) No. 70 Marine Parade (*Crest Hotel*) is a handsome red brick and tile building among the sea front stucco. It replaced standard bow fronts in 1879-80 and was designed by Col. Sir Robert W. Edis F.R.I.B.A., a follower of the 'Queen Anne' school of architecture and friend of William Morris and Norman Shaw, whose influence is evident here.

124.   Western Road before widening in 1903. The domed building on the right still stands at the corner of Clarence Square.

125.   Hove Manor House was, until demolished in 1936, the town's most historic building and the ideal venue for a future museum. The Manor was owned successively by several distinguished Sussex families including the Scraces, Tredcrofts, the Stanfords of Preston and more recently Sir Sidney Granville. The elegant flint house with Adamesque interior decoration was later replaced by Hove Manor flats.

Residence of King Edward VII.
on his visits to Brighton,
Kings Gardens, Hove

126.   In 1908 Edward VII visited Brighton and Hove three times, which did much to revive the
town's fashionable status. He frequently dined with his friend Arthur Sassoon, the rich Jewish
banker, at his house No. 8 King's Gardens (now Royal Court).

127.   Church Road in Hove c.1895, showing the old town hall, a fine terracotta building by Alfred Waterhouse (1882).
It was burnt down in January 1966, and replaced by the present building, opened in 1974. The new town hall, designed
by John Wells-Thorpe, lacks the panache and scale which made its predecessor such an outstanding public building.

Industry

128.   Workers at the Regent Iron Foundry, North Road, c.1900. During the 19th century this and Palmer's Foundry in Chapel Street, Kemp Town supplied material for Brighton's chief projects such as the Chain Pier, Volk's railway and street furniture.

MUTTON'S HOTEL,

Confectionery & Bride Cake Establishment,

KING'S ROAD, BRIGHTON.

WEDDING BREAKFASTS.

☞ *Dinners, Balls, Suppers, Routs, &c., in the most Fashionable Style.*

129. Victorian advertisement for *Mutton's Hotel* showing the interior of the restaurant. The hotel opened in 1820 and remained a popular rendezvous until its closure in 1930.

THE
GRAND HOTEL,

BRIGHTON,

Is situated in the KING'S ROAD, facing the Sea, near the West Pier, South aspect, sheltered from the North and East Winds.

Grand Entrance Hall. Suites of Rooms. Magnificent Coffee, Drawing, Reading and Smoking Rooms *facing the Sea.* Elegant Table d'Hôte Room, also Billiard Room.

High-class Cuisine and Wines. Outside Fire Escapes. Electric Light throughout. Lift for Visitors. Hot and Cold Sea Water, Swimming and other Baths.

———————

Some of the leading Members of the British Medical Association, when staying in the Hotel, certified as to its excellent Sanitary Arrangements.

———————

—— Telegraphic Address: 'GRAND, BRIGHTON.' ——

TERMS 'EN PENSION' FROM 10/6 PER DIEM.

For a period of not less than three days, notice being given on arrival.

———————

Tariff and Full Particulars on application to Mr. A. D. HOOK, Manager.

130. A *Grand Hotel* advertisement published in 1890. The hotel, designed by J. H. Whichcord in an Italian Renaissance style, was erected on the site of the former West Battery House in 1864 at a cost of £160,000. The *Grand* was a leading hotel of its day, with every modern refinement, and its promotion indicates the prosperity experienced by Brighton during the 1860s.

131. Vine Place, a twitten off Dyke Road near Clifton Terrace, commemorates William Vine and the site of his post mill which is shown here. Vine, a leading member of Salem Chapel, Bond Street, died in 1837 and the mill was demolished a few years later.

132. Soper's famous store near the Clock Tower was founded in the early 1860s. The shop later amalgamated with Leeson's and Vokins and finally closed in 1955. Two distinctive domes were added to the building c.1900 and still survive.

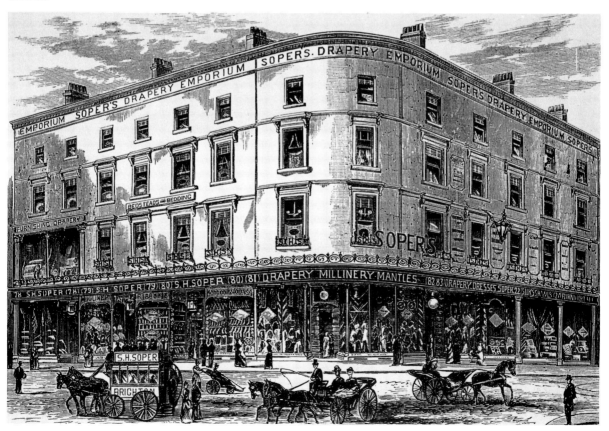

BRIGHTON CORPORATIO

133. In 1882 Magnus Volk devised a private telephone system for his house but it was not until February 1903 that a public service began to operate in Brighton. This view of the Corporation Telephone Exchange was published in 1905.

TELEPHONE EXCHANGE.

S. HANNINGTON & SONS,

SILK MERCERS, &c.,

MAGAZIN
DES
ROBES.

TO HER MAJESTY.

MAISON
DES
NOUVEAUTES.

S. HANNINGTON & SONS

CARPET AND FURNISHING WAREHOUSEMEN,

Cabinet Makers and Upholsterers,

UNDERTAKERS,

2, 3, 4, 5, 171, AND 172, NORTH STREET,

AND 53, MARKET STREET,

2, PAVILION BUILDINGS, AND ROYAL DORMITORIES,

BRIGHTON.

134. Hannington's advertisement c.1870. The store was established at No. 3 North Street in 1802 by Daniel and William Constable who sold out to James Ireland in 1806. In 1822 Ireland opened his ill-fated Gardens with capital gained from selling his shop to Mr. Hannington, founder of the present firm. In 1969 Hannington's was taken over in a £1,000,000 deal by South Bank Estates (London).

People & Events

135. The Triumphal Arch at the North Gate to greet Queen Victoria on 4 October 1837. The Queen referred to the Pavilion as 'a strange, odd, Chinese-looking thing' and, on her visit in 1845 with Prince Albert, the lack of privacy coupled with the 'very indiscreet and troublesome' behaviour of the local people made her decide not to visit the town again.

136. One of the great events in Brighton's history was the return of Queen Victoria in the Royal yacht to the Chain Pier following a visit to the French Emperor Louis Philippe in August 1843. The landing is the subject of a large painting by the Brighton artist R. H. Nibbs, now preserved in Brighton Art Gallery.

137. (*above left*) Lewis Slight (1792-1869) was Clerk to the Brighton Town Commissioners from 1825 until Incorporation in 1854. It was largely due to his efforts that the Royal Pavilion was acquired for £50,000 in 1850.

138. (*above right*) Lt.-Col. John Eld, last Master of Ceremonies of Brighton, who continued in office until 1855, working chiefly from the *Old Ship* and *Castle Inn* Assembly Rooms.

139. (*below left*) Sir John Cordy Burrows (1837-1876), a distinguished surgeon, settled in Brighton in 1835. He was Mayor three times and a statue was erected to him in the Pavilion grounds.

140. (*below right*) Samuel Henry Soper, Mayor of Brighton 1890-91, was a typical self-made man, progressing from a local railway telegraph clerk to ownership of one of Brighton's most successful stores, 'Soper's Emporium', at the top of North Street.

141. The 'Brighton Season' in 1892 depicted with gentle satire by Dower Wilson. Perhaps the most characteristic and fashionable social ritual of Victorian Brighton was the Sunday 'Church Parade'.

142. The first London-Brighton run
entrants at the *Metropole* on 14 November
1896. The run celebrated the Light
Locomotive Act (allowing cars to use
public roads) and of the 54 starters only 13
reached Brighton. The run is now a
popular annual event and open to cars
made before 1905.

143. (*left*) Harry Preston (1860-1936), a Bournemouth hotel proprietor, moved to Brighton in 1901 to take charge of the *Royal York* and, in 1913, the *Royal Albion*. Knighted in 1933, Preston was a keen all-round sportsman and used his influential position to promote and sustain the popularity of Brighton as a leading holiday resort.

144. (*right*) Sir Charles Thomas-Stanford (d.1932), M.P. for Brighton (1914-22) and three times mayor, was described as 'The rare instance of a scholarly man imbued with the enthusiastic public spirit for serving his town and county'. He wrote *Sussex in the Great Civil War* in 1910, and served on the Council of the Sussex Archaeological Society. On his death, Thomas-Stanford's house, Preston Manor, was left to the town as a museum.

SIR CHARLES THOMAS-STANFORD, BART.

145. The well-known Peace Memorial to Edward VII which straddles the Brighton-Hove boundary on the sea front was unveiled in October 1912 by the Duke of Norfolk. The winning design for the £1,000 Memorial was by Newbury Trent.

146. During the First World War, the Royal Pavilion was used as a hospital for wounded Indian soldiers at the suggestion of King George V. In 1915 the King held an investiture at the Pavilion when he awarded the Victoria Cross to Jemadar Mir Dast. Two memorials were erected in Brighton commemorating the Indians: the famous Chattri and the Pavilion South Gate (by Thomas Tyrwhitt), both dedicated in 1921.

147. The dedication of the Chattri Memorial to the Indian soldiers who died at the Royal Pavilion military hospital during the 1914-18 War, by the Prince of Wales (later Edward VIII), on 1 February 1921. The Chattri was designed by an Indian architect E. C. Henriques and marks the *ghat* where cremations took place.

148. 'Some Citizens of Brighton – by Fred May': a page of cartoons of Brighton aldermen and councillors, including Herbert Carden and Harry Preston, published in the *Tatler*, October 1928.

149. (*left*) A local solicitor, Herbert Carden (1867-1941), exerted a formative influence on the development of modern 'Greater' Brighton in the 1920s. Elected alderman in 1903, he became mayor 1916-18, and a freeman of the borough in 1926. He wa closely associated with Louis Cohen in the Brighton & Sussex Building Society and was knighted in 1930.

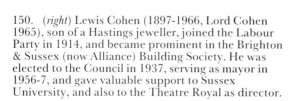

150. (*right*) Lewis Cohen (1897-1966, Lord Cohen 1965), son of a Hastings jeweller, joined the Labour Party in 1914, and became prominent in the Brighton & Sussex (now Alliance) Building Society. He was elected to the Council in 1937, serving as mayor in 1956-7, and gave valuable support to Sussex University, and also to the Theatre Royal as director.

151. North Street elaborately decorated for the Royal Jubilee in May 1935. On the right is the former Countess of Huntingdon church which, until demolition in 1968, gave considerable character to the area.

152. A scene of devastation at Park Crescent Terrace shortly after an air raid in the Second World War. The gap in the Crescent remained until 1984 when it was infilled in exact replica. During the war, Brighton and Hove experienced 83 air raids during which some 300 buildings were destroyed and 227 civilians killed.

Modern Brighton

153.   The Brighton Centre, despite its excellent facilities, bought at a cost of £9 million in 1978, is a ponderous and unimaginative facade – a reversal of the true spirit of seaside architecture. Especially unfortunate is its proximity to the delicate composition of the *Grand Hotel*. The *Grand* is seen here under repair following the disastrous I.R.A. bombing of the Conservative Conference on 12 October 1984.

154. (*above*) In 1935 a large shopping area was proposed near the junction of Western and Dyke Roads but it was 1966-72 before the scheme – Churchill Square – materialised, planned by Russell Diplock. The harsh modern design forms a series of linked piazzas containing some 200 shops plus offices. An abstract sculpture by William Mitchell, 'The Spirit of Brighton', forms an interesting, if ambiguous, focus to the development.

155. (*left*) Brighton Square, completed in 1966 by Fitzroy Robinson & Partners, was exceptional at that time as a development paying some attention to its historical context, particularly in scale. Although the shops are rigid in detail the spire is a pleasant feature, and the scheme makes an honest contemporary contribution to the Lanes area.

156. Duke's Lane (by Stone, Toms & Partners, 1979) may be described as architectural pastiche – a curious attempt to reproduce, at great cost, a random assemblage of late 18th- and early 19th-century buildings of the sort that have been freely pulled down in Brighton and elsewhere for the past 50 years or so!

Dutton & Thorowgood

BOOTMAKERS & IMPORTERS.

CASTLE SQUARE & EAST STREET, *BRIGHTON.*

Western Branch: **94, Church Road.**

· VIEW OF THE PREMISES IN 1837, the whole having been practically re-built during the last Thirty Years.

157.   The old corner house, Castle Square, replaced cottages in 1794-97, and was later remodelled c.1870. In 1985 the new Laura Ashley shop opened on the site. In 1832 the property was acquired by T. Deeble Dutton of Dutton & Thorowgoods and remained a well-known shoe shop for many years.

158.   The new Laura Ashley shop, Castle Square, designed by Nigel McMillan (Hove) in 1985. The building is very successful in being right in scale and context, modern in feeling and yet renews the corner turret tradition, so popular with the Victorians.

159. Stark confrontation between High Rise and Regency in Russell Square – the lasting effects of the Churchill Square development photographed in 1986.

160. A formal Georgian town house is a rarety in Brighton, but this fine example in Prince Albert Street dates from c.1790. Until the 1960s a single-storey shop erected in the early years of the century spoiled the house but this was removed by Mr. E. S. Diplock who purchased the building and restored it as a solicitor's office.

161. (*left*) Black Rock in about 1920 showing the *Abergavenny Inn*, demolished in 1935 when the new sea-wall promenade to Saltdean was begun. In 1963 Henry Cohen proposed a Marina and in 1964 the Black Rock site was chosen. The harbour was opened in 1978 but the controversial commercial and residential development on the site was only begun in 1987. The Marina, despite its leisure and economic advantages, has permanently changed the once beautiful cliff views beyond Kemp Town.

162. (*right*) The east gateway of Queen's Park, South Avenue, refurbished in 1970. The area was laid out as 'Brighton Park' in 1829 by Barry, on land given by Thomas Attree who received permission to rename it after Queen Adelaide. Attree's fine villa stood at the north end (demolished 1974), but the original plan to surround the Park with Italianate villas was never implemented. In 1890 Queen's Park was purchased by the Race Stand Trustees and presented to the town.

163. (*left*)Regency House at the corner of Regency Square was in the 1830s one of Brighton's most fashionable venues when occupied by the Duke and Duchess of St Albans. To the left the new *Bedford Hotel* destroys the scale of the Square and the surrounding Regency buildings.

164. (*right*) The disused Cinescene, North Street, shortly after closure in 1984. The cinema opened in 1911 as the Bijou Electric Empire, but was known for many years as the Princes and Princes News Theatre. The last owner was the late Myles Byrne, also associated with the former Continentale, Kemp Town.

165. (*left*) The well-known Embassy Cinema, Western Road, Hove, just before closure in 1980. Opened in a converted shop in 1910, it became the Tivoli in 1922 and the Embassy in 1950. After a short period as the Black Cat Bingo it has now reverted to being a shop.

166. & 167.   Change at the junction of Queen's Road and North Road. The old print (*above*) shows the elegant Grecian Eye Infirmary (left) designed by Thomas Cooper in 1846, and (right) the former Brighton Dispensary designed by Herbert Williams in 1849 which closed in 1948. The recent photograph (*below*), shows the Eagle Star and other concrete monoliths (c.1960) which have now almost completely replaced the traditional buildings on the east side of Queen's Road. The Eye Hospital moved to Eastern Road in 1935 and the old building was demolished c.1958.

168. *(right)* Advertisement for the old *Princes Hotel*, Hove, now Seeboard Headquarters. Note the words 'Without German or Austrian employees' – it was published during the First World War. The hotel was part of Sir James Knowles' West Brighton Estate and built by a Mr. Prince in 1874.

169. *(below)* The completely refurbished *Princes Hotel*, now Seeboard Headquarters. Work was carried out during 1982-84, and the extension provides an excellent example of adding sympathetically to an older building without sacrificing modernity of feeling. The architects were the Fitzroy Robinson Partnership.

PRINCES HOTEL

BRIGHTON——Grand Avenue, HOVE

The finest position in Brighton

AN ENGLISH HOUSE OF THE FIRST ORDER

An English owned Hotel, without German or Austrian employees
Unique position overlooking the sea and famous Hove Lawns

Magnificent self-contained suites of apartments, with balconies and verandahs facing South and West. Hand——some Lounge and Conservatory——

THE CUISINE IS NOW UNDER THE DIRECTION OF A RENOWNED CHEF

A Choice Stock of Fine Vintage Wines has recently been purchased

Passenger Lifts to all Floors	Excellent Golf Links. Tennis
Sea Water Baths. Motor	and Croquet Lawns, &c. Most
——Garage and Pit——	Modern Sanitary Arrangements

THE DINING ROOM IS OPEN TO NON-RESIDENTS
FOR MEALS TABLE D'HOTE OR A LA CARTE

Hotel Omnibus to   Telephone : Hove 2484
and from Station   Telegrams : " Princes Hotel, Brighton "

170. *(above)* The former Hannington's furniture
depository at the junction of Davigdor and Montefiore
Roads is a distinctive Edwardian commercial building
with a handsome corner domed turret. In the 1970s a
change of ownership led to a complete refurbishment and
internal reconstruction, which conserved the attractive
exterior features.

171. *(left)* New buildings in Manchester Street (1984)
display a commendable awareness of context and scale
and succeed in striking a nice balance between traditional
features – dormers, 'slate', glazing bars – and modern
constructional techniques.

172. *(right)* The concrete mass of Sussex Heights on the site of St Margarets triumphant over the delicate Regency proportions of the remains of Cannon Place. Left is the fine facade of the former Royal Newburgh Assembly Rooms (1825), one of Amon Henry Wild's best compositions, which became the fashionable venue for social life in west Brighton.

173. *(below)* The American Express Building, Amex House, can claim to be one of the most original of Brighton's modern developments. Erected in 1977, on the north side of Edward Street, it was designed by the American architects Gollins Melvin Ward Partnership at a cost of £15 million.

Some Dates in Brighton's History

*c.*3000 B.C.	Whitehawk Camp established.
*c.*250 B.C.	Hollingbury Camp established.
1086	Domesday names Brighton as 'Bristelmestune'.
1313	Market Charter granted by Edward II.
1514	French attack and burn Brighton.
1580	*Book of All the Auncient Customs* published.
1651	King Charles II, following defeat at the Battle of Worcester, escaped to France via Brighton.
1705	Great storm destroyed the 'lower town'.
1753	Dr. Richard Russell established a practice on the Steine.
1761	Brighton population reached 2,000.
	Battery erected at bottom of East Street.
1765	Duke of Gloucester visits Brighton.
1773	Act passed to appoint 64 Commissioners.
	Brighton Camp formed.
1774	North Street Theatre opened.
1775	Old Ship Assembly Rooms opened.
1783	7 September Prince of Wales makes first visit to see his Uncle the Duke of Cumberland at Brighton.
1785	Prince of Wales marries Mrs. Fitzherbert.
1786	Sake Deen Mahomed opened his Vapour Bath.
1787	Marine Pavilion erected by Henry Holland.
1795	Cavalry barracks, Lewes Road, opened.
1798	Royal Crescent begun.
1803	Royal Stables (Dome) begun.
1806	*Brighton Herald* first published.
1807	Theatre Royal opened in New Road.
1815	Death of Martha Gunn.
1817	Trinity Chapel, Ship Street, erected from designs by Amon Wilds.
1820	Mutton's restaurant opened.
	Prince Regent succeeded to the throne.
1822	Charles Augustus Busby (1788-1834), architect, formed partnership with Amon Wilds.
1823	Old Steine enclosed.
	The Brighton Suspension Chain Pier erected by Capt. Samuel Brown.
	Kemp Town development begun.
	Rossini at the Royal Pavilion.
1824	Ireland's Gardens opened at the Level.
1825	Newburgh Assembly Rooms (Cannon Place) built by Amon Henry Wilds.
	The Royal German Spa opened in Queen's Park.
	Amon Wilds appointed Town Surveyor.
	Brighton Town Act passed.
1828	Chantrey's statue of George IV erected in the Old Steine.
	St Peter's church opened.
	Sussex County Hospital and General Sea-Bathing Infirmary opened.
1829	Park Crescent erected by Amon Wilds.
1830	Adelaide Crescent begun.
	Death of George IV on 26 June.
	First visit of William IV to Brighton.

	Town Hall opened.
	Brunswick Square Act passed.
1832	Brighton's first two M.P.s elected: Isaac Newton Wigney and George Faithful.
1836	St Mary's Hall School founded.
1837	Death of Mrs. Fitzherbert.
	Death of William IV.
	Queen Victoria visited Brighton.
1840	Brighton to Shoreham railway opened.
1841	London to Brighton railway opened.
1842	First 'Marina' scheme proposed by George Adolphus Wigney.
1844	Thomas Read Kemp died.
1846	Victoria Fountain opened in the Steine.
1848	Foundation stone of Brighton College laid by Dr. Gilbert, Bishop of Chichester.
1849	Edward Cresy's *Report ... on the Sanitary Conditions ... of Brighton* published.
1851	Thackeray delivered his *Four Georges* lectures at the Town Hall.
	Grand Ball at Pavilion to inaugurate Borough's ownership.
	Electric telegraph installed.
1852	Locomotive works founded.
1854	Incorporation of the Borough of Brighton.
	Major Fawcett elected first Mayor.
1855	Palmeira Square begun.
1856	Brighton Protestant Association founded.
1859	Brighton & Hove Grammar School founded.
1860	French ship *Atlantique* wrecked opposite *Royal Albion Hotel*.
1864	*Grand Hotel* opened.
1865	*Brighton Standard* first published.
1866	West Pier opened.
1872	Sussex County Cricket ground opened in Hove.
	Aubrey Beardsley born at 12 Buckingham Road.
	Aquarium opened.
1873	Hove Commissioners appointed.
1874	St Bartholomew's church, Ann Street, opened.
1876	Sir Albert Sassoon purchased No. 1 Eastern Terrace.
1879	Frank Bridge, composer, born in Brighton.
1881	Royal Alexandra Hospital for Sick Children opened by the Prince and Princess of Wales.
1883	Preston Park purchased from Mr. and Mrs. Bennett-Stanford with the William E. Davies bequest.
	Volk's Electric Railway opened.
1885	Roedean School opened in Lewes Crescent.
1887	Devil's Dyke Railway opened.
1888	The Clock Tower inaugurated.
1889	Brighton gains County Borough status.
1896	Motor-car Day – the first London to Brighton Veteran Car Run.
	Chain Pier destroyed by storm on 5 December.
1898	Brighton United football team founded.
	Incorporation of the Borough of Hove.
1899	Palace Pier opened.
1901	Tramway service opened.
1902	Brighton and Hove Albion Football team formed.
1908	First *Southern Belle* Pullman Express ran between London and Brighton.
1918	Labour first contests Brighton seat in Election.
1921	New South Gate to Pavilion erected by Thomas Tyrwhitt.
	Regent Cinema opened.
1925	Brighton Philharmonic Society founded.
1927	Brighton Corporation Act creates 'Greater Brighton', adding Patcham, Falmer, Ovingdean and Rottingdean.

1934	Dome interior reconstructed.
	Wick Hall, Furze Hill, Hove, residence of Sir Isaac Lyon Goldsmid, demolished.
1936	Hove Manor House demolished.
1938	St Dunstan's Home for blind ex-servicemen erected at Ovingdean from designs by Francis Lorne, F.R.I.B.A.
	Graham Greene's novel *Brighton Rock* published.
1939	Supreme War Council met at Hove Town Hall.
	Tram service withdrawn 1 September.
1940	George VI inspected the invasion defences of Brighton.
1945	Foundation of the Regency Society of Brighton and Hove.
1947	Sir Winston Churchill received the freedom of the Borough.
	Stanmer Estate purchased by Brighton.
1952	Statutory List of Brighton buildings of 'architectural and historic interest' published.
1959	Old Brighton Fish Market closed.
1961	Trolleybus service withdrawn.
	University of Sussex opened at Falmer, designed by Sir Basil Spence.
1964	*Bedford Hotel* burned down.
	Brighton's first Labour M.P., Dennis Hobden, returned (Kemp Town) with majority of 7 votes.
	'Mods' and 'Rockers' riot on seafront.
1966	Hove Town Hall destroyed by fire.
1967	*Dyke Hotel* rebuilt.
	First Brighton Festival.
	Radio Brighton (now Sussex) opened.
1968	Brighton Development Plan approved.
1969	Hannington's Stores (founded 1809) taken over by South Bank Estates Ltd.
1971	Gothic National Schools, Church Street, demolished.
1972	The *Brighton Belle* ran for the last time.
	Death of Herbert Menges, O.B.E., founder-conductor of the Brighton Philharmonic Orchestra.
1973	Hudson Brothers, grocers, of East Street, closed down.
1974	Brighton Borough became a District Council in the local government changes.
	Regent Cinema demolished.
	New Hove Town Hall opened.
	'We Want the West Pier Campaign' inaugurated.
1975	Fire severely damaged the Royal Pavilion music room.
1978	Brighton Centre opened by the Prime Minister James Callaghan.
1979	Brighton Marina opened by Her Majesty Queen Elizabeth II.
1980	*Athena B* aground east of Palace Pier.
1984	Union Congregational church, Queen Square, demolished.
	Conservative Conference at *Grand Hotel* bombed by I.R.A. on 12 October.
1986	Kemp Town Odeon cinema demolished.
	Benjamin Ferrey's St Anne's, Burlington Street, demolished.